Supporting the Move to Whole Language: A Handbook for School Leaders

Supporting the Move to Whole Language: A Handbook for School Leaders

by

Kathy Barclay

and

Elizabeth Boone

SCHOLASTIC

LEADERSHIP
POLICY
RESEARCH

New York ■ Toronto ■ London ■ Auckland ■ Sydney

ISBN 0-590-49222-5

12 11 10 9 8 7 6 5 4 3 2 1   1 2 3 4 5/9

Printed in the U.S.A.

Library of Congress Cataloging-in-Publication Data
Barclay, Kathy.
    Supporting the move to whole language: a handbook for school leaders /
Kathy Barclay, Elizabeth Boone.
       p.   cm.
    Includes bibliographical references and index.
    ISBM 0-590-49222-5
    1. Language experience approach in education—United States–Handbooks,
manuals, etc. 2. School management and organization–United States—Handbooks,
manuals, etc. I. Boone, Elizabeth. II. Title.
LB1576.B296   1993   92-40245
372.6'0973—dc20   CIP

Table of Contents

DEDICATION

To the many, many educators with whom we have worked, we offer our most sincere appreciation. Without you, this book would not have been possible. We also thank the members of our families who have supported us, not only during the writing of this book but throughout our professional careers.

Foreword

When teacher-education institutions and schools collaborate, there is a merging of theory and practice that has long been absent in the educational community. The strong relationship forged by such collaborations benefits the individuals of each institution. From the colleges and universities the schools gain an understanding of the latest research-based theory that is necessary for sound educational decision making. Of equal value are the understandings and insights that the professors gain as the classroom teachers and administrators share not only their classrooms and students but also their informed knowledge of how theory translates into practice.

This book represents just such a collaboration—a melding of theory and research with their manifestations in the classroom and the school. Throughout the book we share both collective and individual experience and insights about whole language . . . about teaching . . . and about educational change. The information shared within these pages represents the best of what we presently understand about implementing a whole language philosophy of learning. We invite you, the reader, to join with us in this collaboration, to mentally share your experiences, questions, solutions, and insights as you read each chapter. By relating a portion of our journey, we hope to challenge others to begin a journey of their own . . . a journey toward whole language instruction.

A Note about the Authors

As an associate professor of elementary education and reading at Western Illinois University and a former classroom teacher and supervisor of reading, Kathy shares with the readers of this book the theoretical underpinnings of a whole language philosophy for teaching and learning, and lends insights into the change process as it relates to instructional settings. Through her work as a national whole language consultant, she has gained a rich understanding of the diversity of whole language teachers and the uniqueness of each teacher's journey toward whole language.

As principal of a K-5 elementary school that has undergone the move toward whole language, Elizabeth brings to the readers of this book the strategies, procedures, and processes that she has found to be most helpful in her work at Oakwood School in Hannibal, Missouri. A respected consultant to both teachers and administrators alike, Elizabeth clearly conveys the critical components found in a whole language school, and shares important insights into how these components might best be developed, evaluated, and maintained.

Understanding Whole Language: The "Whole" Is Greater Than The Sum of Its Parts

A NOTE FROM KATHY....

When, in the twelfth hour of staff development devoted to examining educational teaching practices of whole language, Julie asked, "Do you think I could throw out the weekly spelling lists and develop a spelling program based on the words the children misspell in their writing?" I knew we were finally getting somewhere!

Twelve teachers and I gathered together one evening a month to talk about implementing a whole language philosophy in their elementary and junior high classrooms. When I was first contacted about working with this small rural school staff, I was told, "We already know a good deal about whole language and are trying many new things—but we'd like an opportunity to have you meet with us to help us identify the next steps we need to take."

Before meeting with the group, I asked them to fill out a questionnaire to help me identify what each teacher wanted from our time together. It was fairly obvious from the completed questionnaires that we needed to work toward solidifying our understanding of whole language as a philosophy of education—a philosophy that encompasses far more than just a different way of teaching reading and writing.

While these teachers did have an understanding of and even an ability to apply some of what we might consider the methods or "parts" of a whole language philosophy, they had not, it seemed, come to grips with the notion of whole language in a broader context. Comments such as "I currently teach from the basal in the morning and then do whole language in the afternoon" were not uncommon.

Most of the teachers had abandoned their once-strict adherence to a basal reading program with all its prescribed components. In place of worksheets and workbook pages they used a variety of reader-response activities and trade books to accompany the basal units. Several of the teachers had tried novel units in place of the basal, and one had made a complete transition to novels for teaching reading. With respect to the language arts, a similar movement toward the process approach to writing was evident, although some teachers still relied heavily on the daily lessons prescribed by a commercial language arts text. The kindergarten teachers used a variety of whole language strategies, such as big books and predictable literature. They also encouraged children to use their own invented spellings in creating many of their own books.

As these teachers' methods make clear, we educators are in a transitional state as we seek ways to match our instructional practices with our changing beliefs. As Jerome Harste announced to participants attending the First Annual Whole Language Conference held in St. Louis, Missouri, in August of 1990, "I refuse to apologize for any stage any of you are in—I've been there, too." Just as children who are striving to become readers and writers need time, so also do teachers who are making the transition from a predominantly textbook-driven, subskills approach to a holistic philosophy of learning and teaching. We must give ourselves *permission* to question long-held beliefs and practices and *time* to adopt new ways of being and doing in the classroom.

Whole Language: Philosophy vs. Method

"What exactly *is* whole language?" is a question frequently asked by administrators, teachers, and parents alike. Other questions dealing with methodology, materials, classroom organization and management, and accountability and assessment are usually quick to follow. But while answers to questions about the implementation of a whole language philosophy help explain the "parts" of whole language, they often mask the real issue—whole language as a dynamic philosophy of education.

Frank Smith (1992) states, "The prevailing view in education today is that learning is usually difficult and takes place sporadically, in small amounts, as a result of solitary individual effort, and when properly organized and rewarded" (p. 432). This belief is routinely and unquestioningly perpetuated by the materials we adopt—the basal readers, the language books, the spelling texts, the content-area textbooks, and so forth. When we examine these materials we see that indeed children are given small amounts of information, drill, and practice—over and over again. Textbook sales representatives call this a "spiral" plan because it ensures that children practice the same skill year after year. This approach to teaching only makes sense if you believe that children learn best from isolated, abstract drill as opposed to the meaningful practice of a growing body of skills.

In order for whole language to make any sense, you have to first consider how you think children learn. Then you need to consider how children have traditionally been taught. This is not a simple task. For example, many times teachers and administrators have really not given any serious thought to how they believe children learn to read. When questioned about their reading program they frequently answer with the name of a basal reading company, as though their belief system was purchased right along with the collection of stories and workbook pages! The teaching profession has become increasingly dependent on programmed textbook materials; so much so that we seldom if ever stop to consider whether our practices are in sync with our beliefs. In *Becoming a Nation of Readers* we read that "students spend up to 70 percent of the time allocated for reading instruction in independent practice, or 'seatwork.'" In addition, we are told that "in the course of a school year, it would not be uncommon for a child in the elementary grades to bring home 1,000 workbook pages and skill sheets completed during reading period" (p. 74). This practice persists despite the fact that the majority of workbook pages require only a perfunctory level of reading and that classroom research suggests that the amount of time spent doing these pages is unrelated to year-to-year gains in reading proficiency (Anderson, et al., p. 76). Furthermore, children in the primary grades spend only seven or eight minutes per day in silent reading and only about fifteen minutes a day in the middle grades (Anderson, et al., p. 76). These low figures are despite research findings that "the amount of independent, silent reading children do in school is significantly related to gains in reading achievement" (Anderson, et al., p. 76).

When did we, as professionals, decide that in order to learn to read, a child should spend so *little* time engaged in reading for meaning? And when did we ever *consciously* decide that in order to learn to read, children needed to spend vast amounts of time in paper and pencil tasks that bear little if any resemblance to real, purposeful reading? The answer is "Never!" As professionals we have never made these conscious decisions. Yet because of our lack of commitment to a strong philosophy of education, we have abdicated our role as professional decision makers and have therefore allowed this prostitution of our curricula and our instructional time.

It is precisely the lack of a coherent philosophy of education that too often causes us to jump on the bandwagon when a new program comes along that promises to be all things to all readers. Sometimes, however, in our determination to maintain the status quo we fail to consider new concepts that warrant our careful attention. This reluctance to change often stymies educational progress. One example of this is the continued popularity of "round robin reading." Despite research findings (Durkin, 1987; Gibson & Levin, 1975; Golinkoff, 1975-76; Shavelson & Borko, 1979) linking the habitual use of round robin reading to a dramatic increase in inefficient eye movements, useless subvocalization, and misunderstanding of the functions of both oral and silent reading, teachers still persist in having children follow along silently as poor and mediocre readers struggle through a text, impeding both the rate of silent reading and the comprehension of the listener.

If we are not a nation of readers, it is even more true that we are not a nation of writers. As Lucy McCormick Calkins, noted researcher in writing, said to over five hundred conference participants at the 1989 convention of the National Council of Teachers of English, "The emperor has no clothes!" She explained that during "reading" time in classrooms all across the United States, there is no reading going on. Students are filling in the blanks, underlining, and drawing rings around the best title for the story. Similarly, if we look in the classrooms during "writing" time, there is no writing going on. The students are instead circling nouns, verbs, adjectives, and adverbs. While we want our children to possess this wonderful tool for communicating their thoughts and imaginations, the traditional elementary language arts program rarely includes enough time for children to write for real purposes in a variety of genres. What is produced is often valued more than demonstrated growth in process writing. Further, children rarely write for a real audience or purpose, except for the teacher who grades the finished product. With very young children, writing is often limited to words they know how to spell or copy in a conventional form.

Frank Smith (1988) has shown us that children learn to read by reading and that children will read if they have choices and lots of good literature. One of the most important ways children learn language is by reading and listening to the best that is available. Whole language classrooms are "text rich" places that offer children a wealth of literature to study and appreciate. Children in whole language classrooms are allowed to discover preferences in genres and authors as they are exposed to a wide variety of both. Books offered to very young readers are predictable, rather than simple and boring. Content trade books that make finding information exciting and challenging are used in place of adopted texts that many times are outdated, limited, and uninteresting.

Whole language instruction teaches children the writing process that all good authors use, which includes both a first draft that may contain nonstandard spellings and an emphasis on revising content *before* attending to the form or the mechanics of writing—punctuation, spelling, and grammar. By writing every day, children learn to write and also write to learn. Often the first words that a young child reads are the words that he or she has written. Writing becomes as important as reading, listening, and speaking as children learn to "read like a writer" and to "write like a reader."

It often happens that as teachers begin to try out more and more whole language strategies and experience some success with these strategies, they also begin to feel that something is missing. They realize that there has to be more to this "whole language thing" than they presently understand. This realization, if acted upon in a positive way, leads to real professional growth as teachers start to investigate the power of a whole language philosophy.

Contrasting Models of Education

Traditionally, we have structured our schools, our classrooms, and our instruction according to a transmission model of education (Weaver, 1990). According to this model, the teacher is the imparter of knowledge and the students are the recipients of knowledge and skills. It is the teacher's job to teach and the student's job to learn. Curriculum guides, teacher's manuals, and prepackaged commercial educational materials generally reflect this model. The responsibility for learning falls on the teacher rather than on the learner, in spite of the many typical district philosophies that espouse the development of responsible citizens as one of the primary goals of schooling.

One might ask, "But isn't that the way school is *supposed* to be? Aren't teachers there to teach, and aren't students there to learn?" We find the answers to these questions as we seek to learn how children learn *best.*

According to *Developmentally Appropriate Practice,* a publication of the National Association for the Education of Young Children (NAEYC), "the word 'teach' tends to imply 'telling' or 'giving information.' But the correct way to teach young children is not to lecture or verbally instruct them" (p. 52). The article describes teachers of young children as guides or facilitators (Forman & Kuschner, 1983; Lay-Dopyera & Dopyera, 1986; Piaget, 1972) who pave the way to learning with challenging materials and activities and then step back to observe what the children understand and what further challenges they are ready for. Teachers look for errors, not to "correct" them but to study them, to use them to assess children's learning and to plan future learning experiences. These errors, called "miscues" by Ken Goodman (1969, 1988), are seen as a natural and necessary part of all language learning.

Many common instructional practices work contrary to natural language learning as well as to the creation of life-long readers and learners. To start with, at the heart of our traditional reading programs are basal reading books—collections of excerpts and of stories written specifically to reinforce predetermined skills. As a result, some of the selections included simply aren't that good, particularly at the lower levels where tightly controlled vocabulary results in stilted, unnatural language and sentence structure that often bears little resemblance to spoken language. To children already acquainted with such wonderful stories as Maurice Sendak's *Where the Wild Things Are* and Watty Piper's *The Little Engine that Could,* these "basalized" stories are as unappealing as green beans and spinach. And children who have not had the opportunity to hear a wealth of good children's literature are at an even greater disadvantage because they do not understand what real readers do and lack motivation for "joining the literacy club," as Frank Smith so aptly puts it.

The "basalization" of literature has come under fire recently, particularly with the publication of *Report Card on Basal Readers* (1988), a document detailing the results of a study commissioned by the National Council of Teachers of English (NCTE). In his article "Look What They've Done to Judy Blume! The 'Basalization' of Children's Literature" (1988), Ken Goodman, one of the primary researchers in the NCTE study, compares a basal selection titled "Maggie in the Middle" with the novel on which it was based, Judy Blume's best-selling *The One in the Middle Is the Green Kangaroo.* In the basal version, Freddie, the main character in Blume's novel, becomes Maggie. In Blume's original text, Freddie tries to play with older brother Mike, who tells him, "Get out of the way, kid!" The revised basal version reads, "Go away, Maggie. Run and play with your own friends" (Holt, 1986). Blume describes Freddie as feeling "like the peanut butter part of a sandwich, squeezed between Mike and Ellen," a description omitted in the revised excerpt. As Goodman points out, "The theme of this story, 'it's tough to be a middle child,' remains but it's purged of both the pain and the sibling conflict in the revised version. Just being in the middle is not the same as feeling squeezed between two siblings, 'like the peanut butter part of a sandwich'" (p. 30).

Other problems with our traditional reading instruction abound. Inappropriate practices, as described in *Developmentally Appropriate Practice,* include the traditional reading group routine in which the teacher spends most of the morning listening to students read orally, leading a discussion of a basal story, drilling on skills such as recognizing long and short vowels, and assigning workbook pages and skill sheets to be completed silently by the children. By not being given choices, children do not develop the sense of ownership they need to become self-disciplined, independent learners and responsible citizens. Instead, children frequently are kept together on the same page in a textbook, listening to a discussion that often includes only a small percentage of the students. Thus the teacher's role includes trying to keep the disinterested and unmotivated students involved and on task.

Furthermore, when we use a "basal only" approach, we limit the amount of reading material available to children, "rationing" stories so that the text will last all year. Too often we create the situation described by Nancy Larrick in her article "Illiteracy Starts Too Soon" (1987). There she discusses the "trivialization of reading" that is occurring through the use of prepackaged reading programs containing a myriad of workbook pages, skill sheets, ditto masters, flash cards, and teaching charts, all aimed at teaching children "basal reader language—the only language in print not ever spoken by any human being" (p. 186). As an example of the stilted, unnatural language that so often occurs in basal readers she uses a story in a preprimer book. In the story, Ms. Larrick reports, "ten words are recombined in various ways to result in a twenty-four word 'story'" (p. 186). In the accompanying teacher's manual, 223 words explain how to "teach" the children to read the story.

When I first read Ms. Larrick's article, I could not help but be amused by her choice of stories to include in this article. Only the week before I had observed one of our university prestudent teachers using this same lesson with a group of four first-grade children. Contrary to what we had discussed in our reading methods class, the student had proceeded to ask every question listed in the basal teacher's manual, even though the children told everything there was to tell in their answer to the first question. Naturally, the children began to lose interest in the lesson. As one child poked a second child, a third child asked a question about a picture on a nearby bulletin board, and a fourth child crawled under the table to retrieve a purposely dropped pencil. Needless to say, the prestudent teacher lost her composure and nearly burst into tears as her "by-the-book" lesson fell to pieces—while she was being evaluated by her professor! After three of the four children left for recess (a third had to stay in because he had not completed all of the "seatwork" that had been assigned by the regular classroom teacher), we sat down to discuss the lesson. My first question is usually "What, if anything, would you do differently if you were to teach this lesson again to this same group of children?" Naturally, I expected the student to say that she would not have followed the teacher's manual word for word! Instead, she shared with me her reasons for doing exactly that. As it happened, the classroom teacher had evaluated one of her reading lessons the week before. After the lesson the teacher had said, "I noticed that you left out one of the questions." The student had pointed out that the children had already answered the question in their discussion of a previous question, to which the teacher replied, "Well, don't skip any of them again. There's a reason for *every* question."

This type of thinking undermines the teacher as an instructional decision maker. Rather than view the commercial teacher's manuals as simply guides, many teachers and administrators mistakenly believe that they are "teacher-proof." Teachers like the one my student encountered truly believe that one need only follow the directions exactly to turn out accomplished readers. This "cookbook" approach to reading instruction—not to mention the "bluebird, redbird, buzzard" grouping practices—not only disregards the differences in individual learners but also transforms the teacher's role to that of technician.

As Weaver (1990) suggests, a transmission model of education emphasizes part-to-whole learning. Applied to reading, the model would have us first teach children to recognize the letters of the alphabet, then to associate letters with sounds, then to blend the letters and sounds to form simple three-letter words like *ran, fan, man,* and *cat.* Next the teacher would introduce phrases and simple sentences along with a few "glue" or high-frequency words such as *and, but,* and *the.* Finally, students would begin to read simple stories comprised of about seven phonetically regular words held together by two or three high-frequency words, arranged and rearranged in various ways in an illustrated story of about six sentences.

This is in direct contrast to what Weaver (1990) and others have called a transactional model of education. In this model (Holdaway, 1979; Hall, 1987; Cambourne, 1988; Smith, 1988) the emphasis is on learning from whole to part as "the smaller 'parts' are seen as more readily learned within the context of a meaningful whole" (Weaver, 1990, p. 9). A reading teacher using the transactional model would begin by reading to the children a familiar repetitive rhyme, song lyric, or story. After reading the selection several times she would invite the children to follow along as she pointed to the words and to join in whenever they felt comfortable. Only *after* the children had "read" the simple, repetitive text with her a number of times and had acquired a thorough understanding of the whole piece would she begin to point out the parts that make up the text, such as repeated words and phrases and/or the letters and sounds they are composed of. In this way children learn how reading works—from the top down. That is, they first experience the whole of a meaningful and relevant text, and then they learn about the pieces or parts that make up this whole. Instruction in the mechanics of reading, such as letters, sounds, words, and punctuation marks, occurs after the children understand the text. Thus instruction in each new skill begins and ends in meaningful context. Children are not taught skills simply for skills' sake. Rather, they are taught strategies that anyone, in whatever role or walk of life, can use to acquire and apply knowledge in a variety of real-life learning experiences.

The transactional model is consistent with appropriate teaching practices mentioned in the NAEYC document *Developmentally Appropriate Practice*. For example, this document describes a social studies project in which students develop a plan for building and operating a store. The project gives children focused opportunities to dictate and/or write their plans, to discuss their progress, to read nonfiction books for needed information, to work cooperatively with other children, to learn facts in a meaningful context, and to enjoy learning. The teacher presents skills instruction as needed to enable children to accomplish the project's goals. Children have the freedom to choose from various centers that contain a variety of materials, equipment, and supplies and are allowed the time to use their skills and imaginations to complete their selected task. Thus even very young children in a whole language school are given the responsibility of creating their own project and then of evaluating it with criteria they themselves have set. Older children's time is also less structured and full of choices. Working alone or in small groups, children choose topics, plan projects, and establish deadlines. They are taught early to evaluate their own work and then to improve what they see needs improving. They are challenged not only to answer questions but also to ask questions of themselves and others. Theme study gives children of all ages the chance to ask and answer questions through their research. Information they acquire through this process is internalized and leads to further inquiry. Because children are encouraged to take responsibility for their own learning, a major factor in becoming a responsible citizen is included in a whole language curriculum.

In a whole language school such as Oakwood, the faculty does not assume that children who learn information and the mechanics of language will automatically take their knowledge and skills and apply them to their after-school lives. They believe that children must be shown how the process of acquiring knowledge and skills can be used in the real world and how education will enrich their lives and make them better citizens. As John Holt (1967) states, "If we begin by helping children feel that writing and reading are ways of talking to and reaching other people, we will not have to bribe and bully them into acquiring the skills; they will want them for what they can do with them" (p. 164).

Sound too good to be true? In the video "Why Do These Kids Love School?" Fadiman includes interviews with teachers, administrators, parents, and children from schools across the country. Children in these schools are actively involved in learning. Their learning materials are, as NAEYC advocates, "concrete, real, and relevant to children's lives." Children work with blocks, games, woodworking tools, arts and crafts materials such as paint and clay, and scientific equipment. A variety of work places and spaces, both indoors and out, are flexibly used.

There is a growing number of schools such as these. Two such schools are in Columbus, Ohio. One of them, an inner-city school located in an old three-story red brick building near the campus of Ohio State University, was one of the original "Dewey" schools, known in academia as "whole language" schools even before the term came into being. In both schools the integration of language processes from all areas of the curriculum is clearly evident as students pursue various topics such as change and ecology.

When we hold, however subconsciously, a philosophy of learning that is based primarily on a transmission model, we cannot help but judge each new instructional strategy in light of it. Thus in order to explore and successfully implement new methods of instruction, we must examine our beliefs and openly acknowledge the evolution of models or paradigms. And while we can use many of the parts of whole language, such as big books, the writing process, novel units, and so on, we cannot *fully* demonstrate a whole language philosophy until we consciously embrace a transactional model of education.

Research in Whole Language

Whole language is consistent with the most respected views about how children learn. Theorists and researchers such as John Dewey, Lev Vygotsky, Jean Piaget, and Michael Halliday, to name just a few, have shown that children develop competence in oral and written language while they are *using language* for real purposes. Thus children become proficient language-users despite the absence of direct instruction or isolated skill and drill activities (Goodman, 1989).

The whole language movement stems from Ken Goodman's (1969) work on the psycholinguistic model of reading. However, the movement quickly evolved from a philosophy of reading development to a philosophy of literacy development (Watson, 1982) to a philosophy of teaching and learning (Newman, 1985; Watson, 1989). Whole language research seeks to help educators learn more about how children acquire both understanding of and strategies for living and learning in their world. Whole language researchers attempt to answer questions on a wide variety of issues related to language and literacy acquisition. An abundance of research in early language and literacy development provides a firm base for the whole language perspective. For example, work with preschool children (Y. Goodman, 1990; Hiebert, 1981; Ferreiro & Teberosky, 1982) has yielded important information about children's early awareness of print. In Durkin's frequently cited study of early readers (1961, 1966), she found that preschool children could learn to read naturally, given a stimulating, literate home environment. Similarly, researchers in New Zealand (Holdaway, 1979) and Canada (Doake, 1988) found that preschool children learned to read without formal instruction when they were regularly invited to listen to and read along with good literature. Her research with emergent readers led Clay (1967, 1982, 1991) to conclude that children read more easily when the texts are predictable and of good literary quality. Her research was revalidated when Bridge, Winogra, and Haley (1983) demonstrated that both low-achieving first-grade children and kindergarten children learned more sight words by reading predictable literature than through skill-based basal reading readiness programs. Sulzby's (1985) work with kindergarten readers also revealed that children's reading ability improved from reading storybooks.

In their synthesis of research into the use of "real" books to teach reading, Tunnell and Jacobs (1989) concluded, "The affectivity of literature-based, Whole Language programs gives meaning and pleasure to the process, thus making skills instruction at last meaningful—empowering both teachers and students. At least, it is safe to say the basal reader is not the only way to successfully teach children to read." These authors cite a variety of controlled studies that compare literature-based reading with basal and mastery learning instruction. Studies by Cohen (1968), Cullinan, Jaggar, and Strickland (1974), Eldredge and Butterfield (1986), Larrick (1987), Holdaway (1982), Pinnell, (1986), White, Vaughan, and Rorie (1986), Tunnell (1986), and Reutzel and Cooter (1990, 1992) all report statistically significant gains in reading ability in the experimental literature-based groups over the control groups.

It is important to note that gains in reading achievement from a literature-based approach were not limited to any specific student population. In the studies cited, gains were made by ESL students, students from economically depressed communities, "at-risk" students qualifying for federally funded chapter one services, and average and above average readers.

In one particularly noteworthy study, Ray Reutzel (1987), an associate professor at Brigham Young University, spent a year using storybooks to teach reading skills to sixty-three first-grade children. Deprived of the basals, worksheets, and isolated drill activities typically used in most districts in the state, these students nevertheless learned to read. They read so well, in fact, that all categories of students scored in the 99th percentile on the Stanford Achievement Test, which was administered in March of that year. Every first-grade pupil in the school learned to read, including one whose IQ tested at sixty-eight.

The studies discussed above have both similarities and differences. The similarities are a result of whole language teachers' shared perspective on how children acquire and use literacy skills. The differences result from the empowering nature of a whole language philosophy. Teachers assuming responsibility for instruction means that they rely on their own judgment of how and what to teach and to whom to teach it. This of course results in a wider, more varied, and more personal application of a whole language philosophy.

Whole Language: Common Beliefs

In *What Research Has to Say about Reading Instruction* (Samuels & Farstrup, Eds., 1992), Ken Goodman writes, "In a very real sense, whole language represents a coming of age of educational practice, a new era in which practitioners are informed professionals acting on the basis of an integrated and articulated theory that is consistent with the best scientific research and the theories in which it is grounded" (p. 47).

Teachers of whole language share the view that whole language is a dynamic philosophy of education. The Whole Language Umbrella, a confederation of support groups and individuals dedicated to implementing whole language in the schools, states that the philosophy of whole language embodies

- a holistic approach to all aspects of literacy
- a positive view of all learners

- a belief that language is central to learning
- a belief that learning is easiest when it proceeds from whole to part, when it is in real-life contexts, and when it is useful
- a belief that learning is both personal and social and that classrooms and other educational settings must be learning communities
- an acceptance of all learners and languages and of their cultures and experiences
- a belief that learning is both joyous and fulfilling
  (The Whole Language Umbrella, 1990)

These shared beliefs constitute the foundation of a whole language philosophy. While not unique, they complement the new directions emerging from the various scientific fields. As Paul Drucker (1969) writes, "The fact that we are shifting from a Cartesian view of the universe, in which the accent has been on parts and elements, to a configuration view, with emphasis on wholes and patterns, challenges every single dividing line between areas of study and knowledge" (p. 350). Sam Crowell (1989) alerts us to the implications for education of these changes in scientific thought. Changes in scientific thought include commonly held conceptions about space, matter, force, and the structure of the universe. Developments in virtually every field of science suggests that the universe is a single, dynamic unity, rather than a collection of independent fragments or discrete parts (Prigogone & Stengers, 1984; Davies, 1988.) He challenges us with these questions: "How many educators really believe, based on their experience and observation, that a person learns to read by sequentially mastering 80 to 125 skills in a reading continuum? How many educators maintain that effective teaching is merely the summation of five or seven sets of behaviors organized ideally in linear order? Does anyone actually believe that tests measure what we know? Is knowledge really confined to separate, distinct subjects that rarely relate to experiential reality?" (p. 60). He cites whole language as an approach to language and literacy that "rejects the common separation of language processes into reading, writing, speaking, and listening" and "is an excellent example of many new paradigmatic concepts" (p. 62). These concepts he identifies as integration, complexity, and holism.

Whole language classroom communities ignore many traditional instructional precedents. No longer is the teacher's desk prominently placed at the front of the room. In fact, the traditional teacher's desk is usually the first piece of furniture to be removed in the effort to make more space. Desks are not arranged in rows, as if they were still bolted to the floor. Many whole language classrooms have no desks at all. Tables, benches, beanbag chairs, and study carrels often replace the more traditional schoolroom furnishings. Classroom organization changes, too. Stable ability groupings are out—gone are the "redbirds," the "bluebirds," and the "buzzards." Instead children work alone, in pairs, and in small cooperative groups as part of the whole-class community of learners. In his address to participants of the first Whole Language Umbrella Conference, Don Holdaway referred to the whole language movement as a continuation of the Civil Rights movement. Minorities, women, and now children have rights that need to be respected. Rights of children include an interesting and purposeful education that takes into account individual interests and differences. The skills taught must be applicable to real-life situations that the child is aware of while learning the skills.

Throughout the curriculum, "wholeness" is both created and celebrated as children read and write whole stories and books and solve problems related to many aspects of life, from the possible extinction of the blue whale to world hunger to the importance of rain forests. Reading, writing, listening, and speaking are taught as they are actually used—all day long—to accomplish meaningful and interesting tasks. Students learn the mechanics of spelling, handwriting, and grammar while they write for authentic purposes, such as to convey information about the "save the whale" program, or to write a letter to the editor about recycling, or perhaps to share an amusing personal anecdote with their classmates. Students learn how to read for main ideas and details and to summarize as they read to answer questions they themselves have generated about a topic of interest to them.

It is this coming together of literacy instruction and authentic, real-world tasks that truly makes a whole language classroom "whole." By far the greatest challenge the whole language teacher must face, and face daily, is that of keeping language *whole* while helping students use and deal with its *parts*. While this can be accomplished through a wide variety of strategies, it can be "wholly" successful only after the teacher realizes that the "whole" in whole language is indeed greater than the sum of its parts.

Don Holdaway (1984) has said, "There are no valid reasons for the dismemberment of literacy, only instructional precedents" (p. 3). Rather than worrying about which basal is best or which workbooks and skill sheets to buy, whole language educators struggle with questions such as "How can we integrate the language arts with genuinely important and interesting information about our world and its peoples?" "How important is critical thinking and what are we doing to ensure its integration into all facets of our curriculum?" "What must we do today to help our youngsters not just *survive* but *thrive* in the world of tomorrow?" These are serious issues that merit discussion by administrators and teachers who are struggling to articulate and implement a whole language philosophy.

In order to understand and articulate a definition of whole language, we have to answer a great many questions. Whole language is more than big books, thematic units, and process writing. It is more than cooperative grouping, collaborative learning, learning centers, and projects. It embodies everything that research has discovered about how children learn best, including simple things such as learning by doing, purposeful activities, making choices, good literature, independent reading and writing, sharing, working with a friend, respecting individual differences, learning to evaluate one's own work, and learning from one's errors. In short, whole language is a reflection of the goals that educators have always had for their students. And it is more than the sum of its parts . . . much, much, more.

To reiterate, all schools have goals. In his book *A Place Called School,* John Goodlad (1984) speaks of why we must begin to think in terms of change. "We are not without goals for schooling. But we are lacking an articulation of them and commitment to them" (p. 56). While most districts have stated goals as part of their curriculum guides, if we are honest we will admit that we have strayed from these goals. The National Assessment of Educational Progress (NAEP), an ongoing congressionally mandated project first established in 1969 to determine students' reading and writing abilities, reports that the "overall levels of writing performance remain low" and "the high percentage of unsatisfactory responses and relatively low percentages of adequate and elaborated responses to the tasks described . . . suggest that many students do not possess well-developed persuasive writing abilities—skills that are likely to be important to students in their personal and work lives" (Applebee, et al., 1990, p. 7). Further, the report states that "in general, students appeared to have great difficulty with tasks that asked them to explain or elaborate on what they had read" (p. 7) and that "students' performance was quite low on assessment items that required organizational skills and the ability to synthesize information" (p. 7). About typical classroom instruction the report states that "according to the fourth-grade teachers surveyed, the emphasis in beginning reading instruction in grades 1, 2, and 3 was overwhelmingly on phonics-based or eclectic approaches" (p. 8). In addition, "instruction for most fourth-grade students is based on a single basal reader, with other books and magazines available for supplementary reading" (p. 8). According to the report, higher-level reasoning activities such as discussing, analyzing, and writing about what has been read "are reportedly not emphasized routinely for students" (p. 8).

As we begin to think of what the whole language philosophy offers education today and why we need to move toward changing not so much the curriculum but the way we teach children, we need to be motivated by the realization that present programs do not let us achieve our goals for children. As Applebee states in *The Nation's Report Card* (1990), "Most students' school experiences are dominated by memorization of content presented by teacher or textbook, and by the practicing of skills in workbook or ditto exercises. Students are given limited opportunities to apply knowledge and procedures for new purposes" (p. 35). Similarly, "the need for reform in writing instruction is with us still" (p. 10). Whole language strategies help children attain broad goals; however, these goals cannot be fully realized if they are addressed only by isolated teachers at certain grade levels. Year after year, children must be asked to assume responsibility and to make choices, must be shown that what they learn in school is relevant to the world beyond the classroom, and must come to know the joy that being a life-long learner can bring. Educational leadership's role in this endeavor is critical. Just as teachers must realize that whole language is more than a few new methods and materials, administrators must understand that whole language, when implemented only in isolated classrooms, cannot make the kinds of substantive, lasting changes that are desperately needed. These kinds of changes must spread to every classroom. The principal, as the building administrator working with an enlightened central office staff, can encourage and inspire teachers to reflect on their goals and methods, to implement new strategies, and to refine their beliefs and classroom practices.

References:

– **Altwerger, B., Edelsky C., & Flores, B.** (1987). Whole language: What's new? *The Reading Teacher, 41,* 144–154.

– **Anderson, R., Hiebert, E., Scott, J., & Wilkinson, I.** (1985). *Becoming a nation of readers.* The National Institute of Education, U. S. Department of Education, Washington, DC.

– **Applebee, A.** (1989). *Crossroads in American Education.* The National Assessment of Educational Progress, U.S. Department of Education, Washington, DC.

– **Applebee, A., Langer, J., Jenkins, L., Mullis, I., & Foertsch, M.** (1990). *Learning to write in our nation's schools: Instruction and achievement in 1988 at grades 4, 8, and 12.* The National Assessment of Educational Progress, U. S. Department of Education, Washington, DC.

– **Bader, L., Veatch, J., & Eldredge, J.** (1987). Trade books or basal readers? *Reading Improvement, 24,* 62–67.

– **Blume, J.** (1981). *The one in the middle is the green kangaroo.* New York: Dell.

– **Bredekamp, S.** (1987). *Developmentally appropriate practice in early childhood programs serving children from birth through age 8.* Washington, DC: NAEYC.

– **Bridge, C., Winogra, P., & Haley, D.** (1983). Using predictable materials to teach beginning reading. *The Reading Teacher, 36,* 884–891.

– **Cambourne, B.** (1988). *The whole story: natural learning and the acquisition of literacy in the classroom.* Auckland, New Zealand: Scholastic.

– **Clay, M.** (1967). The reading behavior of five year old children: A research report. N.2.J. *Educational Studies, 2(1),* 11–31.

– **Clay, M.** (1979). *Reading: The patterning of complex behaviour.* Portsmouth, NH: Heinemann.

– **Clay, M.** (1982). *Observing young readers.* Portsmouth, NH: Heinemann.

– **Clay, M.** (1991). *Becoming literate: The construction of inner control.* Portsmouth, NH: Heinemann.

– **Cohen, D.** (1968). The effect of literature on vocabulary and reading achievement. *Elementary English, 45,* 209–13, 217.

– **Crowell, S.** (1989, September). A new way of thinking: The challenge of the future. *Educational Leadership,* 60–63.

– **Cullinan, B., Jaggar, A., & Strickland, D.** (1974). Language expansion for black children in the primary grades: A research report. *Young Children, 29,* 98–112.

– **Davies, P.** (1988). *The cosmic blueprint: New discoveries in nature's creative ability to order the universe.* New York: Simon & Schuster.

– **Doake, D.** (1988). *Reading begins at birth.* Richmond Hill, Ontario: Scholastic-TAB.

– **Drucker. P.** (1969). *The age of discontinuity.* New York: Harper & Row.

– **Durkin, D.** (1961). Children who read before grade one. *The Reading Teacher, 14,* 163–166.

– **Durkin, D.** (1966). *Children who read early.* New York: Teachers College Press.

– **Durkin, D.** (1987). *Teaching them to read.* Massachusetts: Addison-Wesley. 124-147.

– **Eldredge, J., & Butterfield, D.** (1986). Alternatives to traditional reading instruction. *The Reading Teacher, 40,* 32–37.

– **Fadiman, D.** (producer) (1990). *Why do these kids love school?* Pyramid Film & Video, Santa Monica, CA.

– **Ferreiro, E., & Teberosky, A.** (1982). *Literacy before schooling.* Portsmouth, NH: Heinemann.

– **Forman, G., & Kuschner, D.** (1983). *The child's construction of knowledge: Piaget for teaching children.* Washington, DC: NAEYC.

– **Gibson, E., & Levin, H.** (1975). *The psychology of reading.* Cambridge, MA: MIT Press.

– **Golinkoff, R.** (1975–76). A comparison of reading comprehension processes in good and poor comprehenders. *Reading Research Quarterly, 11(4),* 623–659.

– **Goodlad, J.** (1984). *A place called school.* New York: MacGraw-Hill.

– **Goodman, K.** (1969). Analysis of oral reading miscues: Applied psycholinguistics. *Reading Research Quarterly, 5,* 9–30.

– **Goodman, K.** (1992). Whole language research: Foundations and development. In J. Samuels & A. Farstrup (Eds.), *What research has to say about reading instruction* (pp. 46–69). Newark, DE: International Reading Association.

– **Goodman, K., Shannon, P., Freeman, Y., & Murphy, S.** (1988). *Report card on basal readers.* Katonah, NY: Richard C. Owen.

– **Goodman, K.** (1988). Look what they've done to Judy Blume!: The "basalization" of children's literature. *The New Advocate, 1,* 29–41.

– **Goodman, K., & Goodman, Y.** (1979). Learning to read is natural. In Lauren B. Resnick & Phyllis A. Weaver, (Eds)., *Theory and practice of early reading, 1:*137–154. Hillsdale, NJ: Erlbaum.

– **Goodman, Y.** (1989). Roots of the whole language movement. *Elementary School Journal, 90,* 113–127.

– **Goodman, Y.** (Ed.) (1990). *How children construct literacy: Piagetian perspectives.* Newark, DE: International Reading Association.

– **Hall, N.** (1987). *The emergence of literacy.* Portsmouth, NH: Heinemann.

– **Halliday, M.** (1975). *Learning how to mean: Explorations in the development of language.* London: Edward Arnold.

– **Hiebert, E.** (1981). Developmental patterns and interrelationships of preschool children's

print awareness. *Reading Research Quarterly, 16,* 236–260.
– **Holdaway, D.** (1979). *The foundations of literacy.* Portsmouth, NH: Heinemann.
– **Holdaway, D.** (1982). Shared book experience: Teaching reading using favorite books. *Theory into Practice, 21,* 293–300.
– **Holdaway, D.** (1984). *Stability and change in literacy learning.* London, Ontario: University of Western Ontario. Available in the U.S. from Heinemann.
– **Holt Basic Reading** (1986). B. Weiss, E. Everetts, L. Stever, S. Cruickshank, L. Hunt. New York: Holt.
– **Holt, J.** (1967, 83). *How children learn.* New York: Dell.
– **Larrick, N.** (1987). Illiteracy starts too soon. *Phi Delta Kappan, 69,* 184–189.
– **Lay-Dopyera, M. & Dopyera, J.** (1986). Strategies for teaching. In C. Seefeldt (Ed.), *Early childhood curriculum: A review of current research* (pp. 13–33). New York: Teachers College Press, Columbia University.
– **Newman, J.** (1985). *Whole language: Theory in use.* Portsmouth, NH: Heinemann.
– **Piaget, J.** (1972). *Science of education and the psychology of the child* (rev. ed.). New York: Viking. (Original work published 1965)
– **Pinnel, G.** (1986). Reading recovery in Ohio 1985–86: Final report. Technical Report, The Ohio State University, Columbus, Ohio.
– **Prigogine, I., & Stengers, D.** (1984). *Order out of chaos.* New York: Bantam.
– **Reutzel, D. R., & Cooter, R.** (1990). Whole language: Comparative effects on first-grade reading achievement. *Journal of Educational Research, 83(5),* 252–257.
– **Reutzel, D. R., & Cooter, R.** (1992). *Teaching children to read: From basals to books.* New York: Macmillan.
– **Reutzel, D. R., & Fawson, P. C.** (1987). *A professor returns to the classroom: Implementing whole language.* Unpublished research update, Brigham Young University, Provo, UT.
– **Samuels, S. J., & Farstrup, A. E.** (Eds.), (1992). *What research has to say about reading instruction,* Newark, DE: International Reading Association.
– **Shavelson, R., & Borko, H.** (1979). Research on teacher's decisions in planning instruction. *Education Horizons, 57,* 183–189.
– **Smith, F.** (1988). *Joining the literacy club: Further essays into education.* Portsmouth, NH: Heinemann.
– **Smith, F.** (1992). Learning to read: The never-ending debate. *Phi Delta Kappan, 73(6),* 432–441.
– **Sulzby, E.** (1985). Children's emergent reading of favorite story books: A development study. *Reading Research Quarterly, 20,* 458–481.
– **Tunnell, M.** (1986). The natural act of reading: An affective approach. *The Advocate, 5,* 156–164.
– **Tunnell, M., & Jacobs, J.** (1989). Using "real" books: Research findings on literature-based reading instruction. *The Reading Teacher, 42,* 470–477.
– **Vygotsky, L.** (1978). *Mind in society: The development of higher psychological processes.* (M. Cole, V. John-Steiner, S. Scribner, & E. Souberman, eds.). Cambridge, MA: Harvard University Press.
– **Watson, D.** (1982). What is a whole language reading program? *Missouri Reader, 7,* 8–10.
– **Watson, D.** (1989). Defining and describing whole language. *Elementary School Journal, 90,* 129–141.
– **Weaver, C.** (1990). *Understanding whole language: From principles to practice.* Portsmouth, NH: Heinemann.
– **White, J., Vaughan, J., & Rorie, I.** (1986). Picture of a classroom where reading is for real. *The Reading Teacher, 40,* 84–86.

Seeing Is Believing: What to Look for In a Whole Language Classroom

It is, indeed, true that one "sees" based on what one knows, and both the known and the knower are never the same again.

—Yetta Goodman, 1991

In chapter one we compared whole language with a traditional philosophy of education in an attempt to explain what whole language is. We also provided what we feel is a strong rationale for moving away from programs based on a traditional transmission model of education and toward the development and implementation of programs based on a transactional, whole language model.

In chapter two we take a look at the components of a whole language program. Because whole language is a philosophy based on research findings of how children actually learn, strategies for putting these findings into practice are interwoven throughout it. As leaders, principals must have a clear picture of the instruction that should be taking place in each classroom. For administrators in whole language schools, this picture must be based on a thorough understanding of whole language beliefs and practices. Our intent is to help administrators understand what it is they are seeing when they visit whole language classrooms and to point out some things they typically will not see.

Quality Children's Literature

Perhaps the best-known characteristic of whole language classrooms is the use of good children's literature from a variety of genres—fiction, nonfiction, and poetry. Such literature is at the center of the curriculum. And unlike traditional classrooms where basal readers, anthologies, and content-area textbooks comprise the bulk of the available reading material, in whole language classrooms students routinely use real books, magazines, catalogues, encyclopedias, pamphlets, brochures, and so forth. On the average, classroom libraries should have approximately ten books for each child. A core of these books might be permanently housed in the classroom library while the others circulate among the classrooms or go back to a central school, district, or public library. In general, teachers select the books by topic and author, with one goal being to provide a variety of books of different genres and readability levels for each topic or theme children are studying. Students are also encouraged to check out books from other libraries and to bring in books from home. Magazines, travel brochures, pamphlets, and so on are also provided as appropriate.

Rather than rely completely on multiple copies of textbooks, teachers in whole language classrooms frequently buy only a few "reference" copies of content-area textbooks. Additionally, they may select from among a growing body of fine children's literature packaged especially for use in whole language classrooms. For example, some books may be purchased in sets of twenty-five or thirty for use by the whole class, in sets of four to eight for use by small groups, and in sets of two for use by partners.

As we discussed in chapter one, a major criticism of the traditional approach to reading instruction is its use of controlled readers during the early grades. Additionally, the extensive use at all grade levels of excerpts and short stories is seen as a negative aspect of many commercial reading programs. In whole language classrooms, literature serves as a springboard to knowledge in all areas of the curriculum. Even in the earliest grades, children read from whole texts. In this way, students readily come to understand the roles of both author and illustrator and to view writing from the perspective of the reader and reading from the perspective of the writer. It is absolutely impossible for a student in a whole language classroom to "brag" about never having read an entire book. On the contrary, students in whole language classrooms read many, many books throughout the school year.

Whole language classrooms make time for independent reading. Whatever the name—SSR (Sustained Silent Reading), DEAR (Drop Everything and Read, or USSR (Uninterrupted Sustained Silent Reading)—the message conveyed to children is the same. Allowing time for independent silent reading says that reading is what readers do; in fact, it is such an important activity that teachers and administrators do it, too. Children read whatever they like during this important period of the day, whether it be fiction, nonfiction, or poetry in library books, literature study books, or content-area books. While a period for sharing may follow the independent silent reading, students are not required to share, discuss, or give book reports. The only requirement is that they read during the allotted time.

Not only do students in whole language classrooms have many opportunities for independent reading, they also experience a wealth of literature through daily read-aloud sessions. The teacher in a whole language classroom knows that reading aloud to children is an important part of the daily routine. As Frank Smith (1992) says, "The simple act of reading to children serves a multiplicity of vital purposes. It puts children in the company of people who read, shows them what can be done with reading, sparks their interest in the consequences of reading, informs them about the nature of stories, and—most important—puts them in the company of authors" (p. 435).

Listening to good literature also develops children's vocabulary. When children hear interesting words, they begin to use them in their writing. This is shown in figure 2.1, which shows a piece written by Jesse, a second-grader, during the class study of African folktales.

Predictable Literature and Shared-Book Experience

As mentioned in chapter one, at the kindergarten and first-grade levels the literature used to teach reading is very unlike that found in most basal reading programs. Instead of books with ten-sentence "stories" containing only five to ten different words, whole books containing predictable, repetitive patterns, familiar nursery rhymes, poems, chants, and song lyrics initiate the young child into the world of reading.

These reading materials are often printed on large teacher-made charts or in big books—enlarged versions of popular books—that enable children to see the text that the teacher is reading. In the shared-book experience (Holdaway, 1979), the teacher first reads the text to the children and then invites them to chime in on the repetitive portions. The children revisit the same text on subsequent days, now joining in as the teacher points and reads, suggesting words that come next, predicting possible outcomes, and engaging in appropriate expressive activities. After the "experimenting readers" (McGee & Richgels, 1990) have experienced a text in its entirety, they are encouraged to read it independently. The "shared-reading" or shared-language portion of the day typically consists of six parts (Holdaway, 1991). First comes the "tune-in" segment, when children "warm up" by reading or singing short poems, songs, and chants. Next, the children reread several favorite stories. During this time the teacher may suggest activities and ask questions aimed at helping children explore various concepts about print, such as left-to-right progression, spaces between words and punctuation, and at developing beginning awareness of the parts that make up the selection— the syntax, letter-sounds, story structure, and so forth. The third segment of the shared-reading period consists of a variety of language activities such as

Figure 2.1

JESSE'S JOURNAL ENTRY

A Tree That Worked Wonders
by Jesse A. Henoch

One spring morning a girl named Moonlight was walking through the forest. And while she was walking she saw a tree. It didn't look like any other tree in the forest. It just had something different. So she ran to get her mother Sun Dancer. And when she got home she told her mother the whole story. And then she told Moonlight about something that happened to her by the very same tree. This is where the story really starts.

A long time ago, a very long time ago, I was walking through that same forest and something similar to what happened to her daughter happened to her. As I was saying I was walking through that same part of the forest and I saw a hurt squirrel. I ran to see what was wrong. Apparently he'd been shot. I had to move fast or he would die. I bandaged him up as best as I could and I picked him up and I put him in a pouch where he would be safe. On the way I got tired. I sat down beneath a tree. Just then something happened. A bright light came from the tree. It did something because the squirrel was better and running. That made me happy. And I think it was a miracle.

---

playing alphabet and vocabulary games and exploring writing through invented or phonetic spelling. Next comes the "new story" period. During this time the teacher uses unfamiliar text to model decoding and comprehension strategies, how a new piece of text is "unlocked" to obtain meaning. This period is typically followed by an independent reading period, when children are invited to reread, individually or with other children, any of the "old favorites." The children often "play teacher" during this segment, pointing to each word as they reread various charts and books.

The sixth and final segment is the "expression" or independent work period. At this time students work individually or in small groups to extend the story or theme through related arts activities, drama, puppetry, writing, and so forth.

Guided Reading, Reading Workshop, and Literature Study

When students meet with other students and the teacher to read and discuss a selection, they are engaging in what various whole language educators have termed "guided reading," "reading workshop," or "literature study." While basal selections can be used, these strategies typically involve alternatives to the basal reading program.

During guided reading, the teacher usually meets with small groups of students who are reading the same book to discuss their predictions, to share information gained during silent reading, and to practice specific strategies for decoding and comprehending. Guided reading is frequently used during the early grades, when children are just acquiring independent reading strategies.

In reading workshop the students may be reading the same text, or they may be reading a variety of books that are often related by genre or by theme. For example, four students reading mystery stories may meet every day or so to discuss what they have read thus far, focusing on the characteristics of a good mystery story. Or a group of four students reading books related to a unit theme such as change might decide to pair off and read *Roll of Thunder, Hear My Cry* by Mildred Taylor and *The Pearl* by John Steinbeck. When the four students meet to discuss their books, their discussion would center on how the feelings of the characters in the stories change as they encounter racial bias and strife.

At the beginning of each reading workshop, the teacher usually presents a five- to fifteen-minute strategy lesson to show students how to use a specific reading skill. For example, the teacher might discuss ways that a reader can detect character traits, modeling a strategy that involves looking for descriptions about a particular character, noticing what other characters say about the character, and thinking about what the character says and does. Students spend the rest of the period in silent reading, discussion, or response activities such as journal writing.

The teachers at Oakwood base their instruction on literature rather than the basal reader. During literature study, seven or eight children meet with the teacher to read and discuss whole books. As in reading workshop, children choose from among some of the best children's books, and the literature they select may reflect a content-area theme. When the fifth-grade class was studying the westward movement, *Orphan Train, The Cabin Faced West,* and *The Year of the Bloody Seven* were among the available books. Whatever the theme, children are given a wide choice of books so that they will develop broad tastes in books and also be able to find a book they can relate to.

During literature study, the focus is on characters, plot, theme, and all the other components of stories. Teachers at Oakwood feel strongly that the time devoted to literature study should be used to develop children's understanding of and appreciation for literature rather than to dissect isolated pieces of text. Teachers and children read and discuss books in ways they cannot read and discuss the selections in basal readers. Reading an excerpt simply does not promote the involvement that occurs over the length of an entire book. Children in whole language classrooms see the development of plot and character from beginning to end. Consequently, the discussion that takes place in the literature study group broadens and deepens as children get farther and farther into a book.

The problem solving, the oral language, and the depth of understanding that take place in literature study groups create a climate that enables all students to contribute, regardless of their abilities. Children are motivated to read because they are interested in the story and want to participate in the discussion. The discussions are unlike those suggested in basal teacher's manuals, where the emphasis is on checking to see if students have read or can recall the story. Discussions in literature study groups are more like dialogues in which children take the roles of both listener and speaker. Ralph Peterson and Maryann Eeds (1990) call this "a natural way for people to learn and to construct meaning. The lecture model places knowledge outside the students for them to passively receive; dialogue recognizes that knowledge is something students actively construct. Listening to lectures is a solitary activity. Dialogue is a process of co-producing meaning" (p. 21).

Consider this example of the dialogue that took place during a literature discussion in Penny Strube's fourth-grade classroom. The students were discussing *Freedom Crossing,* a story of the underground railroad before the Civil War. Alicia, the group leader, stated her confusion about the word *fugitive.* Her mother had told her that a fugitive was "someone who broke the law." Alicia felt that fugitive slaves should be returned and that people should try to change the law, but that until that happened, slaves should abide by the law. Jackie pointed out that Alicia expressed very different feelings while reading about Jews who ran away from the Nazis.

The above example illustrates the power of dialogue. Such an exchange would never have taken place if the teacher had been directing the discussion according to the questions in a teacher's manual. When children are allowed to assume responsibility for the discussion, they are more likely to make connections both to other literature and to personal experience. Because of the high quality of the literature, children and teachers develop comprehension skills that far exceed those developed when only excerpts or selections with tightly controlled vocabulary are used. Nick, another student in Penny Strube's room, made an important connection during his research on Napoleon. He shared with the class information he had discovered about the possibility that Napoleon had been poisoned by his wife. When an adult listener responded with the opinion that "what had `done' Napoleon in was the same thing that had `done' Hitler in," Nick answered, "Sure, the Russian winters." Nick's knowledge about the two men and the areas and times in which they lived permitted him to make this connection.

Response logs are another important part of literature study. Instead of filling in workbook pages, students think about the text and write their personal reactions to it. As they become engrossed in their reading, their logs become filled with their thoughts about the story. Caleb is a student in Beth Taylor's fifth-grade classroom. His group has been reading *Sh!, We're Writing the Constitution* by Jean Fritz.

Figure 2.2 shows one of Caleb's entries about his reading.

As can be seen from Caleb's entry, he has acquired a great deal of information about this period of history through his participation in the literature study group. Caleb, like the other children in the group, is making connections both to personal experience ("My great uncle worked with or knew J. Edger Hoover"; "I wonder when the F. B. I. started") as well as to other books ("This and *Fredrick Douglass* are in a tie for best of the ones we're reading now").

Strategic Skills Instruction

"But I thought whole language teachers didn't teach skills" is an often-heard comment from individuals who lack a rich understanding of whole language instruction. The fact of the matter is that whole language teachers do teach skills, but they teach them strategically. In a classroom where teaching is based on either a subskills or a skills perspective, one is likely to find a fair amount of instruction in isolated "skills and drills." This means that

Figure 2.2

CALEB'S JOURNAL ENTRY

Shh!   We're Writing
the Constitution

by Jean Fritz

"After the revolutionary war people called themselves "sovereign". That probably means self reign. I like this book~its serious and funny. My two favorite two parts were when Patrick Henry would'nt go to the Con-gressil meeting he said he "smelt a rat." and would'nt go for Virginia. Willie Jones of North Car-olina did'nt say what he smelled but he would'nt go either. (One part I liked about Ben Franklin pg. 11) This gets kind of confusing with all the dates and names. Congress kind of confuses me too. There are three parts to government, legislative, judical, and ex-ecutive. There were fifty-five delegates or congressmen. I wonder when the F.B.I. started cause we're talking about federal stuff. (Federal. Burvo. Investegat-ion.) My great Uncle worked with or knew Jay Ed-ger Hoover (The first leader of the F.B.I.). This and Fredrick Douglass are in a tie for best of the ones we're reading now. The congress could tax the people money, but they did'nt have to pay it. Is this book supposed to be funny? I think projects will be fun for this book. Well I've written a page. What else can I say, I'm drained of stuff to write.

---

the teacher probably uses a commercially published program to introduce skills in a predetermined sequence and then provides isolated practice using skills sheets or workbook pages. The skills seldom, if ever, are linked to a whole piece of text, and students are not usually taught the most appropriate use of a particular skill. Take, for example, the skill of determining main idea. Students being instructed from commercial reading programs are often told to choose the best title for a paragraph or the best topic sentence for a series of unrelated paragraphs. These tasks are not ones that a reader would actually ever do. Furthermore, neither task increases the reader's skill at constructing or creating meaning for a text based on the author's message (main idea), the reader's prior knowledge, and the reader's purpose for reading.

Now let's consider skills instruction in a whole language classroom. First of all, there would probably be _no_ instruction related to "finding the main idea." Why? Because reading in a whole language classroom is seen as a constructive, meaning-getting process; therefore, "getting the main idea" is central to all reading instruction, beginning at the emergent reading stage. Instead, whole language teachers tend to divide skills into three main areas, or cue systems: the semantic or meaning system, the syntactic or grammar system, and the grapho-phonic or phonetic system. According to Goodman (1973), readers use these cue systems simultaneously to predict the pronunciation and/or meaning of an unknown word, and then to either confirm the accuracy of that pronunciation and/or meaning of the word or, when an error occurs, to self-correct the word in order to make sense of what they are reading. Goodman maintains, as do whole language teachers, that "reading requires not so much skills as strategies that make it possible to select the most productive cues" (p. 26). Teaching skills as strategies places the emphasis on applying the skill in a real reading or writing task. Thus, as Routman (1991) states, "The learner must know how and when to apply the skill; that is what elevates the skill to the strategy level" (p. 135).

While strategic teaching of skills certainly seems to make sense, most newcomers to whole language aren't exactly sure how this is accomplished, particularly with respect to decoding skills. If the biggest myth of whole language is that whole language teachers don't teach skills, the next biggest myth is that whole language and phonics are two opposing methods for teaching reading. Again, as we emphasized in chapter one, whole language is not a method for teaching reading, it is a philosophy of education. In fact, we would argue that phonics is not a method for teaching reading, either, but rather one skills component of the reading process. In a whole language classroom, students are taught strategies for working their way through unfamiliar text. They are taught, for example, what to do when they come to a word they do not know. Most students in classrooms where reading is taught as a constructive, meaning-getting process can verbalize a strategy for decoding new words. While the particular language may vary from classroom to classroom, the gist of the strategy is: (1) "I will skip the word and read to the end of the sentence; (2) then I'll think about what word that starts with the same letter would make sense in the sentence; (3) next, I'll try the word in the sentence while looking carefully to see if it has the same letters and parts as the unknown word; (4) if the word doesn't make sense or if it doesn't have the right letters or parts, I'll try another word; (5) if I still can't figure out the word, I'll read on to see if the author gives me any clues as to what the word might be; (6) if I still can't figure out the word but I *can* understand what the author is saying, I can probably skip the word for now and ask about it or look it up later; (7) if I can't understand what the author is saying, I need to stop now and find out what this word is." What makes this strategy so effective is that it is exactly the same strategy that most capable, mature readers use when they come across an unfamiliar word. Furthermore, the emphasis is first on meaning, then on other "cues" or clues such as letter-sounds and word parts. As children become mature readers, they apply strategies such as these as automatically and unconsciously as they tie their shoelaces.

Paula Ingebretson, a second-grade teacher, is at the reading table with Denzil. It is Friday and Paula uses this time to assess individuals on the books they have been reading that week. Denzil is reading his book aloud to Paula, who is evaluating the reading strategies Denzil is using. Denzil pauses at the word *colonies*. He then goes back to the beginning of the sentence and tries to use the sense of the sentence to help him decode the word. Since *colonies* is not in his listening vocabulary, the context doesn't provide much help. Paula helps Denzil use letter-sound clues to decode the word. After he has decoded the word and they have discussed its meaning in the sentence, Paula asks Denzil to recall the strategies that helped him decode the word. By doing so she helps him become consciously aware of good reading strategies. Teachers in a whole language classroom make sure that the children understand that all readers encounter words they do not know, and that *good* readers use strategies that help them unlock these new words.

In the university remedial reading clinic, it is always easy to spot a child who has been in a "phonics-first" reading program. When a child has been taught to overrely on letter-sound relationships to unlock a new word (the "sound-it-out" syndrome), he or she is likely to try to decode a new word without regard for meaning cues or clues in the text. For example, consider the child who is trying to read the word *laughed* in the sentence "'That was such a funny story,' Mary laughed." The child who has been admonished over and over again to "sound it out" will probably pause at the word *laughed* and utter "l . . . l . . . l- a . . . l-a-u . . . l-a-u-g- . . . l-a-u-g-hu- . . .," and so on. Since *laughed* is an irregularly spelled word, the child is unlikely to come up with the correct pronunciation through phonics alone. Meaning clues, such as the context of the sentence, offer a much more effective and efficient decoding strategy, particularly when they are accompanied by *minimal* phonic clues. Therefore, the child who has been taught a balanced decoding strategy would first think, "What would make sense in this sentence? What would Mary do if she thought the story was funny?" The child would then look at the beginning of the word and perhaps think, "Mary would l-a . . . laugh! Yes, that's it! That makes sense."

Certainly there are skills, such as certain phonics generalizations, that when applied routinely help one decode. For example, let's say a teacher decides to use *Curious George Goes to the Circus* during the guided reading time. This book would be appropriate for most second-grade children. The children would already know that the letter c sometimes stands for the sound that *k* makes and sometimes for the sound that *s* makes. They would also know that *g* can stand for the sounds at the beginning of both *goat* and *giant*. Since the phonics generalization pertaining to the hard and soft sounds of *c* and *g* is a very useful generalization and since the book contains a number of words that begin with these letters, the teacher decides to take this opportunity to informally assess which students are and are not able to use this generalization in their reading. By way of introducing the book, the teacher could ask the children what they might see at the circus. The children's responses could be recorded in categories around the word *circus*. Next, the teacher might show a picture of Curious George and ask the children the name of this character. She would write "Curious George" on the board. The teacher might then show the children the cover of the book and ask them to read the title. She might even write a list of words on the board and ask children which words they think might be in a story with this title. In the list she could purposely include words pronounced with both the hard and soft sounds of *c* and *g*, such as *giraffe, goats, guns, games, goldfish, giant, bicycle, unicycle, cannon, acrobat, cotton candy, candy apples, animal cage, cupcake, celery,* and so on. If the children have no difficulty reading the words with the various sounds of *g* and *c*, the teacher might have students make predictions about the story and then start reading. However, if students stumble over the words, the teacher might point out the various words that begin with *c* and *g*. The objective would be for the students to develop the generalization for when *c* sounds like *k* or *s* and when *g* sounds like *j*. The teacher might ask the students to say each word with her and to tell her whether to put an *s* or a *k* over each word beginning with *c* and when to put a *g* or *j* over each word beginning with *g*.

Next, the teacher might help students make four word lists for these four letter sounds. Finally, the teacher would lead the children to discover what the words on each list have in common and to state a generalization that they could apply to unfamiliar words containing *c* or *g*. The generalization would be something like: "When *c* or *g* is followed by an *e, i,* or *y* the *c* makes the *s* sound and the *g* makes the *j* sound; but when *c* or *g* is followed by an *a, o,* or *u* the *c* makes the *k* sound and the *g* makes the *g* sound. As the children read *Curious George Goes to the Circus* they would be challenged to apply the generalization any time they came across a new word containing these letter sounds. They would thus be able to apply the strategy immediately to a real reading task.

Another common concern about skills teaching in a whole language classroom can be stated in this way: "When we use a prescribed skills program, we can be certain that all skills are being covered. How can we be certain of this if we don't rely on a predetermined scope and sequence?" After all, many of us have vivid memories of countless college or university lectures touting the importance of skills! And we recall the strength of conviction with which basal reading company consultants advised us not to skip any of the stories or workbook pages lest we fail to teach a skill needed to read an upcoming selection. As Regie Routman (1991), a noted author and whole language teacher, conveys about her own experience in dealing with this question, "It has taken me many years to become convinced that all the skills are in the literature and that the literature itself can be used as a vehicle to teach skills strategically. I have observed that after about five years or more, teachers seem to move away from practicing specific skills in literature to promoting strategies in the ongoing context of genuine reading and writing, as the need arises" (p. 135).

When teachers first make the transition from teaching isolated skills to teaching strategies for real reading situations, the tendency is to develop "strategy" lessons that are still based on a predetermined sequence of skills. Typically, the transitional whole language teacher uses literature to model a strategy for applying a skill and then encourages students to use the strategy during a similar reading task. While this instruction is literature-based it is not necessarily learner-based. That is, the learners may or may not have a real need for the strategy at the time it comes up in the predetermined scope and sequence of skills. As teachers become more comfortable with teaching strategically and applying skills to a whole piece of literature, they tend to rely less on a predetermined sequence of skills, and more on the literature itself and on their assessment of students' needs. In the long run, many of the same skills will be addressed; however, they will probably not be addressed at the same time, nor will they be addressed with all students. When strategies for using skills are taught when students really need them to accomplish a reading task, they are much more likely to apply the skills to other appropriate contexts. As Routman suggests, "By becoming careful observers of our students and practicing ongoing evaluation, we can determine what strategies students are using and not using. As our own learning theory develops, and as we begin to take ownership of our teaching and rely less on directed instructional programs, we have less of a need for a predetermined skills agenda" (p. 135).

Writing as a Process and as a Tool for Learning

When we use what we know as professionals about how to teach children to write (Graves, 1983 & 1989; Calkins, 1990; Harste, Short & Burke, 1988; Atwell, 1987 & 1989), the writing process becomes paramount in a whole language classroom. It is the glue that holds much of the curriculum together. It plays a major role in teaching the mechanics of writing—phonics, grammar, punctuation, spelling, handwriting—that have traditionally been taught as isolated skills during what was referred to as language arts. Further, it serves as a powerful learning tool since it requires students to organize, synthesize, and clarify their thinking about various topics. In a whole language classroom, writing is not taught through workbook pages or skill sheets. Children do not "practice" placing quotation marks, commas, and end punctuation in sentences written by someone else. Teachers do not group children for writing instruction. All students begin with only pencil and paper, which enables the teacher to assess each individual learner and provide appropriate instruction.

When teachers and children view writing as a process, they expect to develop a piece of writing in stages. The process begins with *thought* as children mentally plan what they are going to write about. Teachers frequently encourage prewriting techniques such as brainstorming, reading, interviewing, outlining, and webbing to help children organize their thoughts and get them on paper before they begin to create a first draft.

The children then create a *rough* or *first* draft of their paper. This draft is usually shared with a small group of classmates, who give the writer "audience feedback" about the piece. This constructive criticism may comment on the subject of the piece, what the listener liked about it, what he or she did not understand or would like to have had more information about, and so on. The student author uses this audience feedback to make decisions about future drafts or *revisions* of the piece.

After addressing content, the student focuses on form or mechanics. During this *editing* stage, the revised piece is read aloud by a "co-editor," who is responsible for helping the student author find and correct errors in punctuation, grammar, and spelling. Finally, the edited piece goes to the "editor in chief" (the teacher), who makes any additional editing suggestions before the student author prepares the final version.

Throughout the writing process the teacher schedules several conferences with each student. The conferences may last as long as ten to fifteen minutes or as little as a minute or two. During these conferences the teacher might help the student plan a new piece of writing, give an on-the-spot minilesson of a skill the student needs for her or his writing, or simply check to see that the student's writing is moving along through the process.

The last stage of the process is the *sharing* stage. During this stage students may share their completed work in any number of ways, including publishing their writing by binding it in book form, reading it to the entire class, including it in a class anthology, or framing or mounting it and displaying it on a class or school bulletin board.

Children in a whole language classroom are asked to write in every area of the curriculum. They use their journals to tell the teacher about their personal lives—their thoughts, feelings, and actions. Figure 2.3 shows an entry of Katie's, in which she tells her first-grade teacher, Mrs. Davis, about a frightening event that took place at her house.

During their literature study, students use writing to organize their thoughts and to respond to their reading. In figure 2.4 Kirk, a student in fifth grade, makes some predictions about what he thinks will happen next in the book *Frederick Douglass;* later he makes connections between various historical figures.

Children's writing takes many forms. Figure 2.5 shows a poem written by Natalie during her second-grade class's science-related theme study.

Integrated Curriculum and Theme Study

Perhaps one of the most distinctive characteristics of many whole language classrooms is the absence of the artificial curricular boundaries that characterize traditional classrooms. For example, whole language teachers view the processes of listening, speaking, reading, and writing as simply that—processes for using language. This is in direct contrast to classrooms where listening, speaking, reading, and writing are taught as separate curricular areas. It is also quite a contrast to classrooms where reading is divided into components such as phonics, oral reading fluency, and comprehension, and writing is divided into spelling, handwriting, composition, and grammar, with each often being graded separately. In fact, in a whole language classroom the language processes are not viewed as subjects at all, but rather as ways of gaining and sharing information about oneself and one's world. Hence, students in whole language classrooms are both immersed and engrossed in thematic units of study in which they use the language processes to discover and share answers to a variety of questions. The theme is the foundation on which meaningful and purposeful

Figure 2.3

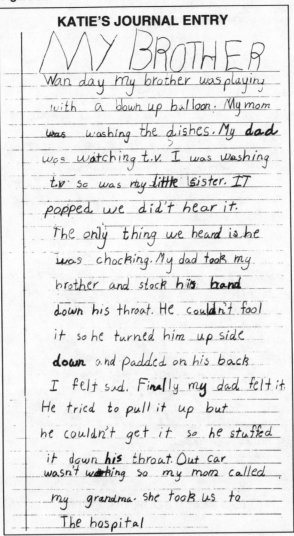

KATIE'S JOURNAL ENTRY

MY BROTHER

Wan day my brother was playing with a blown up balloon. My mom was washing the dishes. My dad was watching t.v. I was washing t.v. so was my little sister. IT popped we did't hear it. The only thing we heard is he was chocking. My dad took my brother and stock his hand down his throat. He couldn't fool it so he turned him up side down and padded on his back. I felt sad. Finally my dad felt it. He tried to pull it up but he couldn't get it so he stuffed it down his throat. Out car wasn't working so my mom called my grandma. she took us to The hospital

study takes place. Through theme study, students accomplish authentic tasks requiring them to strategically apply specific knowledge and skills.

At Oakwood, the entire curriculum is driven by themes, large subject areas chosen because of the interest they hold for children. A theme may be science- or social studies-related; it could be as broad as "U.S. Conflicts" for fifth-graders or as narrow as "Spiders" for first-graders. The themes may even reflect a mandated curriculum, if one exists. For example, at Oakwood themes cover the subject matter listed for each grade level in a statewide curriculum guide. Children at one grade level are required to study regions of the United States. Teachers at that grade level typically involve the students in a study of Native Americans, a theme that both lends itself to a

Figure 2.4

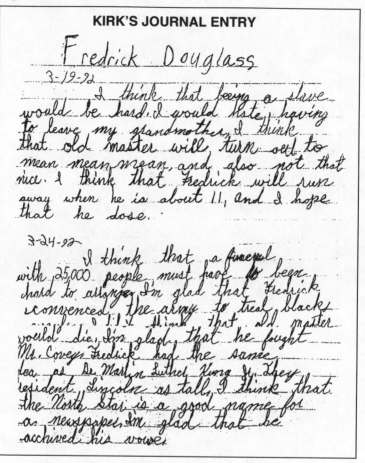

KIRK'S JOURNAL ENTRY

Fredrick Douglass

3-19-92

I think that being a slave would be hard. I would hate having to leave my grandmother. I think that old master will turn out to mean mean mean, and also not that nice. I think that Fredrick will run away when he is about 11, and I hope that he dose.

3-24-92

I think that a funeral with 25,000 people must have to been hard to arrange. I'm glad that Fredrick convenced the army to treal blacks equal. I like him that old master would die. I'm glad that he fought Mr. Coveys Fredrick had the same idea as Dr. Martin Luther King Jr. They resident Lincoln as tall. I think that the North Star is a good name for a newspaper. I'm glad that he achived his wowe.

Figure 2.5

NATALIE'S JOURNAL ENTRY

Eagal

The eagal,
Golden as the setting sun,
Soaring over the land,
Until the golden sky fades away,
And then night will fall,
A dark, booming blue.
Stars as bright as dimonds
Apear in the deep, indago sky.
Nothing can be heard but the soft,
Swish, swish, swish
Of the wind.

study of *all* of the regions and encourages investigation into the natural resources, history, climate, animals, and animal habitats of each region. There are many other themes that could also include study of the regions of the United States. The choice of theme varies from classroom to classroom and from grade to grade. Sometimes teacher and children collaborate in choosing the theme. Teachers who give students some of the responsibility for theme planning find that they become very wise curriculum planners. As Schwartz and Pollishuke (1991) state, "When the planning of an integrated, child-centered curriculum is done with the children and by the children, the experiences become more relevant, because they are built on the backgrounds, interests and everyday life experiences of each individual student" (p. 50).

Another name for theme study is theme cycle (Altwerger, Edelsky, & Flores, 1987). As one unit or theme is drawing to a close, the teacher and children begin to develop plans for the next. The new theme may arise from the children's desire to pursue information they learned from the earlier theme. Such was the case in Peggy Veatch's second-grade classroom. A theme study based on African folk tales, which the children began in February, turned into a study of slavery, which evolved into a study of black awareness, which led children to write biographies of Abraham Lincoln, Martin Luther King, and Thomas Jefferson, among others.

In many classrooms books and resources related to the next possible theme in the cycle are made available even before children complete the present theme. The teacher may also use bulletin board and poster displays to promote interest in a possible theme. Themes are frequently arrived at when the students engage in a brainstorming technique in which they think about what they already know about a topic and then read further in order to collect as much information as possible before they embark on a full-scale unit of study. The teacher begins this process by displaying a giant "web" on the overhead screen or chalkboard. The plan of study begins to evolve when the children answer such questions as "What do I already know about this topic?" and "What do I want or need to know about this topic?"

When children are given frequent opportunities to become involved in theme planning, they begin to realize that they are being given the power to plan activities that they will carry out over the next several weeks. They actively participate in making choices about what they want to learn about, what their responsibilities as researchers will be, what the end products will look like, what the criteria for evaluating the products will include, and how they will share what they have learned with an audience.

As teachers become skilled at facilitating thematic study, they begin to promote research techniques similar to those that might be used by "experts." For example, as Jerome Harste (1991) states in the foreword to his book *Creating Curriculum,* "If the topic I'm interested in is `immigration' I ask myself questions such as `What would an anthropologist want to know about this topic? What would a biologist contribute? What would a psychologist want to know?'" (Foreword). From such questions evolves an up-to-date curriculum that is purposeful, meaningful, and relevant.

The curriculum that is organized around a theme takes on an entirely new look. Teachers are no longer dependent on a textbook that gives only a little bit of information about a great many topics; rather, the resources the class uses, including trade books, magazines, videos, newspapers, people of the community, encyclopedias, and other reference materials, provide abundant information about the subject. Consequently, teachers no longer complain that children can't read the textbooks. Children choose materials that are on their level and beyond, because they need and want the information a particular resource offers. When the students are aware of what they need to know and to be able to do, they become very responsible learners.

Similarly, as teachers begin to realize the power of theme study, they move beyond the traditional "read-and-write-a-report" type of assignment. Rather, they encourage a variety of activities that enable students to explore and share the topic. For example, a product of a "Wild West" theme could be a newspaper for which the children, acting as reporters, write articles that describe the development of the West for readers back East. The theme of "Fossils" could have as its product a geologist's field notebook. While studying water the students could learn (through research, videotapes, filmstrips, class discussions, simulations, experiments, field trips, guest speakers, and so forth) about water's role in weather, about the properties of water, about various bodies of water (including where they are located and how they affect the people of the area), about the water cycle and the importance of water conservation, and about how people, animals, and plants use water. The recreational uses of water, such as swimming, boating, skiing, and scuba diving, could then be explored, which could lead children to learn about water safety.

During the unit the students would constantly be using language—listening, speaking, reading, and writing—to learn about water and to share what they have learned. For example, they could write informational essays comparing and contrasting fresh and salt water animals; practice narrative and share weather facts by writing a script for a weather report using new vocabulary words like *precipitation;* write personal narratives and free verse to convey feelings associated with swimming, scuba diving, or other water activities; combine persuasive writing skills with letter-writing skills in composing a letter to the editor of the local newspaper to persuade citizens not to throw tin cans and other debris into the park pond; draw a map showing the locations of various bodies of water in the city and state; develop and illustrate "how to" essays about water sports; and write postcards to a class partner to share factual information about a particular body of water.

Throughout the water unit, the students would develop their knowledge, skills, and attitudes relative to all language processes and all subject areas. Even math skills could be included as students calculate the longest and shortest distances across various bodies of water and how far they live from various lakes, rivers, and oceans. Problem solving and cooperative learning would be stressed as students plan guest speakers and field trips as well as other activities. As Australian educator and author Diane Snowball (1992) explains, "Through participation in such events, students learn both the processes and content which may be related to more than one curriculum area at the same time. There's a goal to achieve, providing a focus for the learning. Along the path to that goal, the activities interweave the processes and content from various curriculum areas. Always, there's an authentic learning situation that establishes the focus and purpose of the learning" (p. 54).

Each child gets a chance to be the "expert" for a portion of the theme study. The children know that as experts they will be responsible for sharing their information with the class. Class presentations are thus an intrinsic part of each unit. As the presentations are made, class members listen attentively, take notes, and formulate questions. Many times these presentations are videotaped so that students can review the information. Parents may also check out the videos, thus serving as yet another audience for the budding public speakers. An added benefit from making presentations an integral part of the unit is that it enables the teacher to assess both listeners and speakers.

For a final evaluation the teacher usually asks students, even very young ones, to answer the questions they posed at the beginning of the theme cycle. Older children may be asked to respond in essay form. For example, Beth Taylor asked her fifth-grade students to pretend they were living during the American Revolution and to write letters to the future children of America. The class decided that the letters must include facts about the war, the government, and the people of the time. Figure 2.6 shows Carrie's letter, in which she identifies our country's first elected and appointed officials and explains the judicial system.

In a whole language classroom integrated learning is more than the use of "across the curriculum" activities aimed at connecting a particular topic or work of literature to various subject or curricular areas. It is more than simply having fifth-grade students write book reports about novels set during the Civil War as part of a social studies unit. It is more than having first-grade students recite poems about snakes and make clay snakes during a unit on snakes and other reptiles. Instead, the activities are derived from purpose or focus questions that students and teacher pose at the beginning of the unit. Thus, as Snowball suggests, "The focus questions are the driving force, and the purpose of doing any of the activities is to answer the focus questions" (p. 55).

To illustrate this point further, several years ago "letter of the week" programs, which still persist in many kindergarten classrooms, became popular. Instead of subdividing the kindergarten day into various curricular

Figure 2.6

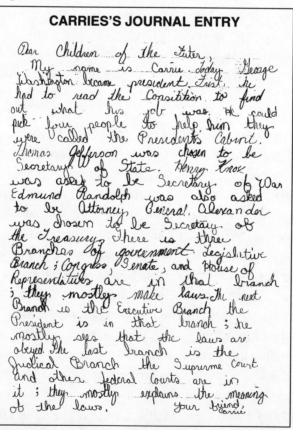

CARRIES'S JOURNAL ENTRY

Dear Children of the Futer,
My name is Carrie. Today George Washington became president. First he had to read the Consitition to find out what his job was. He could pick four people to help him they were called the Presidents Cabinet. Thomas Jefferson was chosen to be Secretary of State. Henry Knox was asked to be Secretary of War Edmund Randolph was also asked to be Attorney General. Alexander was chosen to be Secretary of the Treasury. There is three Branches of government. Legislitive Branch; Congress, Senate, and House of Representatives are in that branch; they mostley make laws. The next Branch is the Executive Branch the President is in that branch; he mostley sees that the laws are obeyed. The last branch is the Judicial Branch the Supreme Court and other federal Courts are in it; they mostley explains the meaning of the laws. Your friend, Carrie

or subject areas, teachers of these programs planned lessons that integrated the entire curriculum around a particular "letter of the week." For example, when the letter *b* was introduced, the children read stories about bears and birds, glued beans and birdseed onto construction paper cutouts of pictures whose names started with *b,* played with balls of various sizes, painted with blue and brown paint, used blue playdough, counted bluebirds, balls, and bears in math, and perhaps even cooked and ate brownies. But while these activities, like whole language activities, relate instruction to a common element, they are primarily teacher-directed rather than child-centered or learner-directed. When children, even five-year-olds, are allowed to decide what they want to know more about or learn how to do, they will often reveal an astonishingly wide range of interests. For example, one group of kindergartners asked about the ocean, "Why is it salty?" "How do plants grow in the ocean?" "Why can't you see the salt?" "Why doesn't the whole ocean evaporate to make rain?" "Why do ocean plants need more water than plants on the ground?" Another group wanted to know about cats. When the teacher asked what they already knew about cats, they responded with a list of facts that included:

1. Cats have kittens.
2. Cats chase mice.
3. Cats have claws.
4. Cats can climb trees.
5. Lions and tigers are related to cats.

Their list titled "What We Want to Know about Cats" included: "How many different kinds of cats are there?" "Who are a cat's enemies?" "What do cats eat?" and "Are there cats all over the world?"

Children will seldom, if ever, tell you that they have a burning desire to know more about the letter *b.* Nor will they usually reveal a desire to know more about turkeys, Santas, snowmen, or hearts—our typical holiday fare for early childhood units of study. To state it simply, children want to know about their world and everything in it. Their desire to learn is insatiable, and their powers of retention are amazing. Whole language teachers take advantage of these qualities by listening to children talk about what they are interested in, finding out what they already know about a particular topic, and arranging the environment so that it provides ample opportunities for independent and collaborative learning, thinking, and problem solving and promotes the skills and strategies needed to accomplish desired tasks.

In Closing . . .

Educators often use the word *community* when they are talking about whole language classrooms. The word is generally used to describe a special feeling in a classroom where the children and the teacher work together in a spirit of cooperation and mutual respect. Whole language teachers create a democratic society that respects and recognizes the rights of everyone. All children respond positively to this treatment. Many teachers think that a class's ability to work together for a common purpose depends a great deal on the "luck of the draw." However, from our frequent observations of whole language classrooms, we have come to realize over the years that they all soon become communities. They all develop that feeling that comes only when everyone's abilities, needs, and interests are being considered and met. When teachers feel that their classrooms are communities of learners it is evident to administrators, parents, and children.

Frank Smith (1992) states, "The problem is that teachers, parents, and administrators often cannot distinguish the desirable from the deplorable. There is a greater need for sensitivity than for new information, for willingness to explore than for determination to hold a position" (p. 441). As administrators we not only have to look for signs of community, we have to be actively involved in its development.

What whole language offers administrators are strategies and tools that they can explore with teachers to help make each classroom a place where learning and teaching are productive and interesting. Administrators need to take note of and encourage strategies that promote active language learning through purposeful content study. In the next chapter we will describe strategies for becoming actively involved in your school's effort to change.

A Postscript from Elizabeth . . .

When the fifth-grade teacher became ill and I had to take a bus of thirty-two fifth-graders to visit Lincoln Land in Illinois, I experienced firsthand what theme study meant to the curriculum. The field trip was one of the culminating events for a study of the Civil War period. We were early for our visit to the Lincoln home and were to wait in the souvenir shop for our guide. I thought it might be a long, dull wait, but I needn't have worried because the shop was full of interesting artifices, books, and memorials about the Civil War. I told the children that if they could spend it wisely, I would let them have $50.00 from our school funds to buy research materials for next year's fifth-grade students.

We could have spent two hours instead of just one! They knew what they were looking for. We bought copies of the Gettysburg Address, the Emancipation Proclamation, diagrams of battlefields, and many wonderful resource books. Serious negotiation took place as the students exhibited not just knowledge of facts but a deep comprehension and a genuine interest in the subject. It was a delightful and enlightening day!

References:

– **Altwerger, B., Edelsky, C., & Flores, B. M.** (1987). Whole language: What's new? *The Reading Teacher, 41(2),* 144–154.

– **Atwell, N.** (1987). *In the middle.* Portsmouth, NH: Heinemann.

– **Atwell, N.** (1989). *Coming to know.* Portsmouth, NH: Heinemann.

– **Calkins, L. M.** (1990). *Living between the lines.* Portsmouth, NH: Heinemann.

– **Goodman, K.** (1973). Psycholinguistic universals in the reading process. In F. Smith (Ed.), *Psycholinguistics and reading* (pp. 25-26). New York: Holt, Rinehart and Winston.

– **Graves, D. H.** (1983). *Writing: Teachers and children at work.* Portsmouth, NH: Heinemann.

– **Graves, D. H.** (1989). *Experiment with fiction.* Portsmouth, NH: Heinemann.

– **Graves, D. H.** (1989). *Investigate nonfiction.* Portsmouth, NH: Heinemann.

– **Harste, J. C., Short, K. G., & Burke, C.** (1988). *Creating classrooms for authors.* Portsmouth, NH: Heinemann.

– **McGee, L. M., & Richgels, D. J.** (1990). *Literacy's beginning.* Boston: Allyn & Bacon.

– **Peterson, R., & Eeds, M.** (1990). *Grand conversations: Literature groups in action.* New York: Scholastic.

– **Routman, R.** (1991). *Invitations.* Portsmouth, NH: Heinemann.

– **Schwartz, S., & Pollishuke, M.** (1991). *Creating the child-centered classroom.* Katonah, NY: Richard C. Owen.

– **Short, K. G., & Burke, C.** (1991). *Creating curriculum: Teachers and students as a community of learners.* Portsmouth, NH: Heinemann.

– **Smith, F.** (1992). Learning to read: The never-ending debate. *Phi Delta Kappan, 73(6),* 432–441.

– **Snowball, D.** (1992). Whole language: The authentic classroom. *Teaching pre K-8, 22(8),* 54–56.

CHAPTER THREE

No One Ever Said That Change Was Easy: Understanding and Fostering Changes In Beliefs and Practices

There is much greatness in our public schools . . . we must work together to show that picture and at the same time make change where it is needed.

Thus states a 1991 report of the Illinois Association for Supervision and Curriculum Development Think Tank, which convened in June of 1991 "to identify pressing issues and to brainstorm ideas that will open new educational opportunities or improve upon those that are already in place for the people of Illinois" (p. 1). The participants in that meeting challenged public schools to "unleash the power of teachers" and to "focus educational efforts toward individuals, recognizing their unique talents and potentials, rather than emphasizing stereotypes which may guarantee failure or hinder the development of self-actualized, self-sufficient individuals" (p. 2).

Similar groups of individuals are convening in schools and school districts all across the United States as well as in many other North American countries. Terrence Deal, in his article "Reframing Reform," which appeared in the May 1990 issue of *Educational Leadership*, cites a number of schools and districts that are examining past and present educational values and practices. Among those listed are the Fairfax County Public Schools, Virginia; Todd Elementary School in Briar Cliff, New York; the Edina, Minnesota, public school district, and the Caldwood Elementary School in Beaumont, Texas. What these and many other schools such as Oakwood School have in common is a collective commitment to reshape schools in order to better prepare youngsters for the world of tomorrow. In his article Deal states, "For the most part, efforts to improve public schools have concentrated on correcting visible structural flaws. However, deep structures and practices cannot be reformed; they have to be transformed" (p. 9).

We believe, as Deal suggests, that teachers, schools, and school systems that truly wish to implement a whole language philosophy of learning must be *transformed* rather than *reformed*. Transforming schools takes time. As Deal observes, "Transforming schools entails a fundamental renegotiation of cherished myths and sacred rituals by multiple constituencies: parents, local politicians, or residents, as well as administrators, teachers, staff, and students" (p. 9). Well-designed programs that develop community awareness and staff competency are a critical part of this effort at transformation.

In an article that discusses the effectiveness of networks in providing an alternative to traditional staff development activities, Ann Lieberman and Milbrey McLaughlin (1992) describe four characteristics that successful networks share. These are: (1) focus, or a clear sense of purpose and a sense of identity among individuals who pursue common interests and objectives; (2) variety in professional growth opportunities and a blending of personal and professional, social, and work-related activities; (3) discourse communities that encourage, foster, and empower teachers as knowledgeable decision makers and risk takers; and (4) leadership opportunities for teachers willing to share their ideas with other teachers through such activities as workshops and writing for publication. "In this period of intensive school reform, when traditional inservice training and staff development have been shown to be inadequate," these authors contend, "networks can provide fresh ways of thinking about teacher learning" (p. 677).

The development of networks is a central part of the whole language movement. The Whole Language Umbrella offers support and networking services to members. Often described as a "grass roots" movement (Goodman, Bird, & Goodman, 1991), whole language has typically been initiated by teachers who are trying to transform their classrooms and schools. In her article "How to Start Your Own Grass-Roots Whole Language Organization" author Lillian Hentel of Tucson, Arizona, emphasizes the importance of "commitment to whole language, lots of publicity, teamwork, and the courage to take risks" (p. 413). In addition to these elements, Nancy Areglado and Laurel Stevick recommend a "team approach" involving various schools within the network and encouraging group members to "bring materials and ideas to share" (p. 413).

A NOTE FROM KATHY . . .

Networking, sharing, and risk taking are critical components of the whole language movement. Yet not all teachers "come to whole language" in the same way (Goodman, 1991). Not surprisingly, there are many, many "practicing" whole language teachers who are basically alone in schools where textbook-driven curriculum and isolated skills instruction are the norm. To illustrate this point, consider these statements made by Margaret Harn, an outstanding first-grade teacher who participated in a graduate course that involved a commitment to "make a substantial change in your present classroom/school situation." Margaret teaches in a school where she is one of only a very few whole language teachers. Both the kindergarten and second-grade teachers are *traditional "by the book, basal reader" teachers. In a discussion of past versus present beliefs and practices, Margaret told the other seven members of the group, "I have been `basal-less' for three years! Oh, my, this sounds like TRUE CONFESSIONS! I can't go back . . . it's hard for someone else to understand—it's hard to explain. Something has to give—I can't go back—I won't!"*

The administrator plays a critical role in promoting and supporting changes in beliefs and teaching practices. A question that teachers frequently ask is "How can I get my principal to let me do this?" Given building administrators' high degree of accountability, it is certainly understandable why a principal may be reluctant to issue a go-ahead if she or he does not fully understand the request. Enlightenment is the key. As administrators at all levels come to understand what whole language is all about, their reluctance will gradually fade.

As we state in our conclusion to chapter one, substantial, lasting change is only really successful when all classroom teachers share a compatible philosophy of learning. While changes are often implemented one teacher and one classroom at a time, the thoughtful administrator will actively seek ways to initiate whole-school improvement efforts.

Noted educators, researchers, and authors Ken Goodman, Lois Bird, and Yetta Goodman (1991) describe what whole language means for school administrators:

> Whole language means new roles for supporting teaching and learning. It means curricular leaders who provide resources, who facilitate holistic planning, and who help teachers evaluate teaching and learning to produce continuous growth in both. Whole language administrators are not afraid to put their trust in teachers and learners, and they're not afraid to take risks themselves to change traditional piecemeal schools to holistic integrated ones. Whole language administrators lead a collaboration of professional educators, parents, community members, and students to create schools that are dynamic learning communities. (p. 4)

The remainder of this chapter is devoted to a discussion of the role of the thoughtful administrator in not only supporting a grass roots movement toward whole language but also in assuming an active leadership role in transforming a school into a dynamic, whole language center for learning. We will share with you strategies for initiating changes and for empowering teachers to become risk takers and decision makers. We will also describe qualities of effective staff development activities and suggest a list of topics on which to base district or school inservice programs. The strategies we will share come from our own experiences. They are our "stories" about how a whole language philosophy of learning has been implemented in various classrooms and schools. In telling our stories, we are ever mindful of Ken Goodman's admonition to whole language educators not to take a "wholier than thou" stance with teachers who are moving slowly into a whole language program (Goodman, 1986). Just as we recognize and value the individuality of children and their various rates of learning, so too must we respect the individual differences of the teachers and administrators with whom we work.

Moving Toward Whole Language: What We Have Learned from Research

In the past fifteen years or so we have seen a fair amount of research concerning teacher change. Much of the research has stemmed from studies of "effective" schools. In looking at differences in effectiveness among schools, Datta (1980) found that changes in the teachers' own behaviors accounted for improvement in student performance more often than did number of years as a teacher, teacher effectiveness, or support for inservice training. Yet changing the way teachers teach is a very involved process. Meyer (1988) emphasizes the magnitude of the task involved in changing beliefs and behaviors:

> First, we expect them to change behaviors. Even simple behavioral changes are difficult to achieve. When we ask or demand that teachers change how they teach, particularly when new techniques are different ideologically and behaviorally from those they learned and accepted in college, we are asking for what Kuhn (1970) called a paradigm shift. (p. 56)

In their article "Linking Classroom and School Improvement," authors Fullan, Bennett, and Rolheiser-Bennett describe a framework for systematically linking three main areas: classroom improvement, teacher development, and school improvement. The authors subdivide these three areas into four interrelated aspects. The *classroom improvement* area consists of content, instructional strategies, instructional skills, and classroom management; the *teacher as learner* area consists of technical repertoire, teacher as researcher, collaboration, and reflective practices; and the *school improvement* area includes collegiality, shared purpose, continuous improvement, and structure. The authors state that while individual classroom, school, and district needs and conditions will generate a variety of options, districts will benefit from attending to all of the components. Additionally, they state:

> Innovations should be seen as points of departure or catalysts, rather than as things to be implemented. Innovations, even major reforms, because they are by definition temporary, can be

diversions rather than aids to fundamental, long-term change. The problem of seeking innovations as solutions is acute because decision makers are so vulnerable to "quick fixes," given the political and time pressures under which they work. (p. 19)

Ample staff development opportunities, necessary curricular materials, and time for implementation must be accompanied by a solid understanding of the changes to be made and the various levels of use through which teachers progress as they begin to implement classroom changes (Hall, Loucks, Rutherford, and Newlove, 1975). These levels range from *nonuse* and *orientation,* when teachers are only beginning to learn about new practices; to *preparation* and *mechanical* use, when teachers plan how to incorporate new strategies and actually attempt to master the day-to-day use of them; to *routine, refinement, integration,* and *renewal,* which are characterized by a stable use of the strategies, integration and coordination with other teachers, and exploration of modifications or alternatives aimed at improving the new strategies. It is virtually impossible for a teacher not to progress through these various stages or levels of use when attempting to change classroom practices. Oftentimes it is when a teacher reaches the "mechanical stage" that the administrator begins to hear comments like "This isn't working for me," "This takes too much time!" "I'm spending so much time in planning and preparation that I don't have enough time to teach!" or even "O.K., I've given this a try, now I'm going back to the way I did it before." When this happens, the administrator must be ready to: (1) help teachers realize that their feelings and concerns about management issues are absolutely normal, and (2) provide additional support, perhaps in the form of classroom aides, release time, and so on, to help teachers progress through the stages of change.

When a master classroom teacher gets involved in a major effort to change, support from the administrator or from an outside consultant is especially important. This may be because the master teacher—a teacher who has experienced a great deal of success—is suddenly placed in a role that is like that of a novice teacher. Not a very comfortable place to be! A few years ago, a similar situation evolved with a fifth-grade teacher who was attempting to "shelve the textbooks" and teach reading and language arts through the use of novels and content area materials. Late in October the teacher threw up her hands in frustration and said, "This is taking too much time! I haven't covered nearly the amount of material that I usually cover by this time of the semester!" This outburst was somewhat of a surprise, although it certainly shouldn't have been, since the teacher was merely expressing where she was with respect to the change process. We talked about what *had* been accomplished, in terms of both her own understanding of the new strategies and that of her students. Earlier that semester she had bemoaned that "these students don't know how to discuss a book—they only know how to fill in a worksheet!" Now, after just two months of participating in book discussions, the students were asking higher-level questions about what they had read and stating and justifying their own opinions based on information from the book and/or from prior knowledge. This represented a major accomplishment, and one that students in previous years had not had the opportunity to pursue. As we continued to discuss the stages through which everyone involved in any change process naturally progresses, she felt more at ease and willing to persevere in her efforts at change.

According to Gallagher, Goudvis, and Pearson (1988), when teaching is the target of change, two key issues must be considered: individual teacher input into her or his own professional development and the anticipated outcomes of the particular change. Additionally, Carnine (1988) stresses the need for teachers "to be coached to behave in new ways before they believe the new methods are worthwhile" (p. 27). This coaching can take many forms. Teachers might be encouraged to try out a new strategy for just a week or two and then report the results in a faculty meeting or in a conference with the administrator. Charleen, a third-grade teacher who decided to stop using worksheets, skillsheets, and workbook pages for one week, tells this story:

> The children worked with a reading partner. One day I listed several questions on the board and asked the children to select one question to answer. They read all of the questions. There was discussion between the children as to which question each student would answer. Not one set of reading partners answered the same question. Where were all the students that looked across their neighbor's desk to fill in the blanks on the worksheets?
>
> This experiment really made me evaluate the large amount of time that we spend on worksheets, and the validity or non-validity of these worksheets. It appears that I have relied too heavily on worksheets in the past. I hope I will be more selective with the use of this type of activity in the future, and will teach for concepts and ideas—not for activities. (Barclay, 1991, p. 61)

Empowered Principals . . . Empowered Teachers

For a building-level administrator to effect any substantive and lasting changes, she or he must first be empowered by the district office and the school board to make decisions based on the strengths and needs of teachers and students. This includes the power to: (1) interview prospective teachers for that school, (2) work with teachers to implement up-to-date programs that are consistent with schoolwide beliefs, goals, and objectives, (3) recommend transfers for teachers who would prefer *not* to teach in a whole language school, and (4) empower teachers as curriculum designers, staff developers, classroom researchers, and professional decision makers. Even in schools such as Oakwood where management is site-based, an enlightened central office staff is needed to help sustain the changes that are taking place in the school. The district-level administrators are, therefore, critical players in the creation of a whole language school.

In *Getting Reform Right: What Works and What Doesn't,* Fullan and Miles (1992) state, "Change requires the power to manage it" (p. 751) and "Successful change efforts are most likely when the local district office is closely engaged with the changing school in a collaborative, supportive way and places few bureaucratic restrictions in the path of reform" (p. 751). Superintendents, curriculum coordinators, supervisors, and school board members must be informed participants from the outset because through their active involvement and support, school-level administrators become infinitely more able to promote positive and lasting changes. When district-level administrators are open to learning about whole language as a philosophy for living and learning, principals and teachers are more likely to get the materials and staff development opportunities they need to develop and implement a whole language program. Furthermore, district-level administrators are in a better position to support the move toward whole language when they understand exactly what teachers and principals believe and are trying to do. Changes involving the evaluation and documentation of pupil progress, parent and community involvement, textbook adoption policies, and a wide range of other critical issues can be more effectively made when everyone in the school system shares a common knowledge base and system of beliefs with respect to whole language.

Acquiring this common knowledge base and belief system is not as difficult as it might at first appear. This is largely because whole language, when systematically explained and demonstrated, makes sense, even to noneducators. For example, when you say that you want students to read whole books instead of only excerpts from books, you receive very little argument. Your suggestion that many and various resources rather than just one text be used to teach social studies and science is most often met with hearty approval. When you say that students should be involved in daily sustained writing experiences rather than in simply filling out workbook pages, agreement is universal. Whole language makes sense, but because it represents a new way of thinking and doing—a change—it must be fully explained to everyone involved in the decision-making process.

An empowered principal strives for change, not by mandate, but by promoting and actively supporting teacher involvement in the change process. This means empowering teachers to discover what whole language means to them and how they can best implement a whole language program with their students.

A NOTE FROM ELIZABETH . . .

It was the summer before I began my tenure as principal of Oakwood, and I was attending the Mark Twain Literacy Conference with some of the teachers that would be in my building. We were coming together for a large group meeting after attending several of the conference sessions. Penny Strube sat down next to me and said, "Can I do this?" Penny had just come from a session led by Kittye Copeland, a whole language teacher from Columbia, Missouri. Penny had difficulty believing me when I told her that she certainly could do what she heard Kittye saying about her program. Penny was thinking about all the textbooks from which she had always thought she had to teach. She was thinking about all of those workbooks that were waiting for her and her fourth-grade students at Oakwood. She was thinking about past practices regarding grouping students for instruction and about the Core Competency and Key Skills that were mandated by our state testing program. Penny must have asked me the same question about five times that day, because even though she was a veteran teacher, she had always followed the teacher's manuals that accompanied the district-adopted curricular materials. She had always viewed as her responsibility "covering" the information in those texts. Penny was not an empowered teacher.

There are teachers like Penny in virtually every school—teachers who are dissatisfied with what is happening in their classrooms and who realize that many of the things that they are doing are not working as well as expected, are inefficient, or are disliked by the children. These teachers simply need permission to plan their instruction around the needs and interests of the children.

The first step in empowering teachers is to decide with the staff that the teachers must have permission to plan and develop instruction that is developmentally appropriate for the children. Often this first step is enough for teachers to initiate plans, attend workshops and classes, visit other classrooms, and assume responsibility for their own instructional program.

Teacher empowerment does not mean that shared goals and objectives are cast aside. Rather, it means that each teacher accepts responsibility for merging children with the curriculum in the way that she or he deems most appropriate. This is in sharp contrast to a system or school where there is the general assumption, either conscious or unconscious, that responsibility rests more with the adopted textbooks and materials than with the classroom teacher. For example, in one graduate class the students were asked to survey their fellow teachers in order to obtain information about curricular changes. One student asked her colleagues if they changed their program each year to accommodate the individual students in their class. Over 85 percent of the teachers in one building answered that they did not make these kinds of changes—that their program remained basically stable unless they themselves switched grade levels, in which case they followed the teacher's manuals for that grade level.

The principal's function as instructional leader takes on a new dimension—that of being a colleague with teachers who are ready to implement changes in their classrooms. Both principal and teacher need to have a clear picture of what the classroom should look like. This shared picture should include both the goals to be achieved and the skills to be gained, as well as explicit agreement about children's interests, their appreciation of literature, and the need for their active involvement in purposeful reading, writing, and research. The teachers plan the instruction and organize the classroom to achieve the outcomes, while the administrator acts as a facilitator and a resource person who observes and offers feedback as the changes are taking place.

Some teachers, however, are hesitant to give up the comfort and security of a teacher's guide or manual that tells them what to do and often what to say. These teachers *can* become whole language teachers, but more effective and efficient ways of living and learning in the classroom must be demonstrated to them. They must experience lesson by lesson that children can and do make good choices and that they will do the children more good if they relinquish some of their control and allow the children to assume ownership of and responsibility for their own learning.

These teachers, too, must be involved in developing the goals for implementing changes in their own classrooms. Further, to ask teachers to change everything they do in the classroom at once would be so overwhelming that they would have little chance of succeeding. Effective administrators, serving as change agents within their own buildings, will help teachers identify those practices already in place that are consistent with the research in whole language. They will then help teachers formulate plans for initiating changes step by step.

We have found that literature study is generally a good place to start to change classroom instruction. This is because children respond very quickly to reading good literature in its entirety. Besides, motivating children to read is much easier when "real books," rather than the basal reader, are used. Teachers making this change do so with the understanding that children become better readers by actually reading and that one of their goals is to increase the amount of reading that children do. The teacher will probably make a gradual transition into the use of literature for teaching reading. Perhaps the teacher will continue to use a supplemental "skills program" until he or she becomes convinced that teaching reading strategies *as students need them* the reading of a piece of literature is more effective. Initially, the discussion periods will probably resemble those that take place following the reading of a basal reader selection—the teacher asking questions primarily to make sure the students completed the reading assignment. Later, as the teacher becomes more knowledgeable about various discussion strategies, these discussion periods will become more like dialogues or what Peterson and Eeds call "grand conversations" (1990) focusing on higher-level thinking skills and the creation of new insights.

In many classrooms the writing process is one of the first whole language strategies implemented. The goal in these classrooms is to teach children to communicate their thoughts in writing. Even though teachers realize that filling in the blanks on workbook pages does little to produce better writers, they are often at a loss as to the best way to teach writing, particularly to a classroom of twenty-five or thirty students. Implementing a process approach to teaching writing generally requires the teacher's involvement in staff development activities. At first these may focus the teacher on helping the children move through the stages in the process—planning, drafting, revising, editing, and sharing—of writing, for example, a personal narrative. Later, as the teacher and students get a better understanding of the writing process, they will apply this understanding to a variety of writing tasks. At this stage the teacher unfailingly begins to realize that the traditional exercises in grammar, punctuation, and spelling are not efficient, because students learn these mechanics much more easily when they use them in their own writing.

When working with individual teachers to set goals for moving toward whole language, thoughtful administrators will need to take into consideration the components already in place in each classroom. For example, since theme study requires strong literature and writing components, goals pertaining to integrating the curriculum with thematic unit development are usually not the first ones to be addressed. Later in this chapter we include a list of various topics that are often explored, through staff development offerings, during the planning and implementation of a whole language program. Recognizing that there are individual differences with respect to the move toward whole language, we offer these topics only as examples of the many that might be addressed.

Administrators empower teachers when they ask for and listen to teachers' views, when they invite teachers to participate in decision making, when they trust teachers to develop a curriculum of their own that is compatible with school philosophy, and when they ask for teacher input into how school funds can best be spent. When teachers become less dependent on textbooks, money formerly used to buy those books and accompanying materials such as ditto masters and workbooks can be used to buy trade books and research materials to use in social studies and science, multiple copies of literature to use in study groups and reading workshop, and predictable literature and big books to use during shared and guided reading periods, to name but a few of the many resources that complement a whole language program.

At Oakwood, many of our materials are stored by theme in crates kept in our resource room. These crates typically contain a collection of trade books (both fiction and nonfiction), posters, videos, software, models, children's reports, and anything else that might help children study that particular theme. A text crate on "Bugs" could include butterfly nets, mounted specimens, filmstrips, Eric Carle's books *The Very Hungry Caterpillar, The Very Busy Spider, and The Very Quiet Cricket,* copies of magazines like *Ranger Rick, In Your Own Backyard,* and *National Geographic,* as well as field guides and other research books. Resources like those stored in our text crates help teachers plan and implement thematic units. When these resources are not available, the teachers spend a great deal of time gathering materials to use during a particular unit of study.

Textbooks and ancillary materials are generally quite costly. Giving teachers access to the funds that were once used to purchase these materials is a critical step toward empowering them as curriculum planners and decision makers. With this new empowerment, teachers become very selective about their purchases. They usually find that many forms of instructional materials are less expensive than textbooks and their accompanying materials. The care and thought that go into making these purchases usually means that money is much more wisely spent.

Through this empowering process teachers such as Penny Strube begin to trust their own professional judgment. They stand up for what they believe, and they articulate supporting evidence based on their knowledge of research and of children as active, constructive learners. Such is the case with Louise, a kindergarten teacher who states:

Most of the other teachers in the primary wing feel that allowing invented spelling fosters bad habits that result in poor spelling grades. Since I'm the "new kid on the block" I have little chance of converting them to my philosophy, but I now feel that I'm on solid ground in my thinking. Taking graduate classes and reading articles defending the support of invented spelling have empowered me to stand up for my allowing its usage in my classroom.

Making the Move: A Transitional Process

In chapter one we emphasized the importance of articulating one's philosophy or beliefs about learning. Ronald A. Christ and Diane H. Nettles (1992), both from California University of Pennsylvania, PA, have developed what they call a "measuring stick" for teachers to use in evaluating how far they have traveled "on the road to whole language." The purpose of their inventory, which consists of twenty statements of teacher behaviors to which teachers are to respond with *always, sometimes, rarely,* or *never,* is to indicate whether a teacher is practicing most, many, or few whole language strategies. Some statements reflect whole language strategies, such as "I use themes that are integrated in all subject areas." Others consider more traditional, subject-oriented strategies, such as "I teach spelling and/or language lessons each day or a few times a week" and "Textbooks are used and assignments are given in the sequence as shown in the manual." The authors stress that the measuring stick is aimed at helping classroom teachers and is not to be used by administrators to evaluate.

A similar inventory was developed earlier by Diane DeFord, professor of education at Ohio State University. The DeFord Theoretical Orientation to Reading Profile (TORP) (1987) helps teachers identify where they are with respect to a whole language philosophy of teaching reading. In her inventory DeFord includes twenty-eight statements about reading instruction to which teachers respond by marking SA for Strongly Agree, A for Agree, N for Neutral, D for Disagree, or SD for Strongly Disagree. For example, item number ten reads, "It is a good practice to correct a child as soon as an oral reading mistake is made." Teachers follow the directions for scoring the inventory and then plot their score along a continuum to discover their "dominant perspective": subskills, skills, or whole language.

This inventory can serve as a starting point for a discussion about beliefs regarding whole language. After a period of study including, perhaps, attending inservice workshops, reading professional literature, visiting whole language classrooms, and viewing videotapes about whole language, teachers may want to respond to the statements again to detect any changes between past and present beliefs that might have occurred. In the discussion that follows, Pam Campbell compares her pre- and post-inventory scores:

My initial response is "Wow, what a difference!" I remember doing the preclass inventory and feeling very indecisive. I found myself reading and rereading several of the statements, in an attempt to clarify their meaning.

The postclass inventory took little or no time to complete. I felt so strongly about each issue that I didn't need to reread hardly any of the statements. I have changed my dominant perspective from a score of 97 with skills as my perspective to a score of 120 which indicates a whole language perspective. The style of my classroom reflects this change as well. Children learn more from interaction and trial/error than they do from my instruction; therefore, I find myself becoming more of an observer/navigator than the dominant leader I used to be. This has made teaching more enjoyable for me and I'm sure the students enjoy their day more as well. Recess is no longer the only opportunity for interaction in my classroom.

Joan McDearmon, an excellent preschool teacher, tells about her "old" beliefs about the reading process and the changes she has made that were revealed by her "post-inventory" score.

Slightly over three months ago the area of "Skills" was my dominant perspective. Now whole language is. I previously believed that skills and drills were needed practically before we even put a book in a child's hands, and certainly before we ever expected him/her to read it. Reading, to me, was the perfect pronunciation of each word. I guess I just assumed comprehension magically followed good oral reading. Largely through class lectures, I have come to realize that even though we can read a passage aloud very accurately, it does not mean that we understand it.

Yes, I have a way to go before fully implementing all I have learned in this course, but I have changed so much in my philosophy and practice in just three months that I am very pleased with my professional growth. I am also pleased that I now am no longer just a facilitator, but a knowledgeable one, and I feel much more competent in guiding children down the path of emergent literacy.

Sometimes the inventory can raise many questions for a teacher who is beginning to make the transition to a whole language perspective. Such was the case with Andrea McVey, a first-grade teacher who shares her feelings after comparing her pre- and post-inventory scores:

I find it hard to believe that my score increased fourteen points when I feel "shaky" about whole language! I feel that I have been handed a 1000-piece puzzle with no interlocking grooves or picture to follow and then have been told to "put it together yourself!" My training and experience some years ago wasn't completely traditional, but a whole language philosophy was never mentioned.

Despite my insecurities, I know that eventually I will be able to put all the pieces of the puzzle together in the correct order. Maybe someday with a few more reading classes on my transcript I will be able to send you a note that says, "I did it!"

Using Performance-based Teacher Evaluation as a Catalyst for Change

We have emphasized the importance of providing ample time to plan and implement desired changes. Lasting, substantive changes cannot take place overnight. Teachers cannot be asked to completely abandon past practices until they are sure that the new ones are at least as effective as the old ones. They cannot in good conscience give up their workbooks and skill sheets until they are convinced of the validity of children's using writing and other literature extension activities to respond to their reading.

At the same time, however, administrators need to assess whether changes that have been agreed upon are, in fact, being implemented in a timely and appropriate way. One New Zealand teacher attending a conference in Chicago was overheard telling a group of American teachers, "We have a saying: `If you're green, you're growing. If you stop, you rot!'" Most of us have had the unfortunate experience of being in the midst of a "rotting" change effort. The administrator must assume responsibility for conducting ongoing evaluation of the change effort and for intervening should a breakdown in the process occur.

Chapter 7, "Staying Whole: The Importance of Professional Growth and Development," covers specifics concerning the implementation of a performance-based system for teacher evaluation. Since this approach to evaluation is flexible and multifaceted, it can serve dual purposes. With respect to change, performance-based evaluative procedures make it easier to identify strengths and needs that would affect the implementation of a program compatible with schoolwide philosophy, goals, and objectives. Working with teachers to set goals for their classrooms, administrators strive to take the risk out of change by advocating a step-by-step approach, establishing a generous time frame, and providing feedback, support, and encouragement. Additionally, when the entire school is involved in the move toward whole language, the process is easier simply because everyone is undergoing some degree of change at the same time. Teachers are then more open to sharing not only books and other resources but also experiences, successes, and even failures. Interestingly, when the whole school is involved the children experience the changes also. Their enthusiasm is often contagious, causing some reluctant teachers to feel a certain pressure from the noticeable enjoyment of children in other classrooms. This pressure, which may also come from parents who recognize the power of a whole language classroom, must be dealt with carefully so as to avoid a polarization that would interfere with a smooth schoolwide transition to whole language. Some teachers will change at a much slower pace than others, but with a supportive administrator, increased resources, and performance-based teacher evaluation techniques even the most reluctant teacher will begin to make the move.

Becoming Whole: Implementing a School or District Plan for Moving Toward Whole Language

While recognizing that no significant changes in paradigms or belief systems can be mandated or implemented all at once, we believe that a knowledgeable and thoughtful administrator can successfully navigate a school toward a whole language program. The research is certainly clear about the need for change, and the stage has been set by the grass-roots movement toward whole language.

In the preceding sections we discussed research into effective change efforts, emphasizing the active roles of both teacher and administrator in transforming classrooms and schools through changes in beliefs and practices. In this section we share suggested guidelines for writing a school or district plan for a whole language program. We also discuss effective staff development practices and recommend steps and topics for a school or district staff development program.

CREATING ACTION PLANS.

Designing and implementing a whole language program involve a great deal more time, energy, and commitment than does textbook adoption, which primarily involves the acquisition of a product. As discussed earlier in this chapter, creating whole language programs involves changing long-held beliefs and practices. Since this change is a process to be implemented rather than a product to be acquired, ample time for planning must be provided. In order to facilitate the process, the administrator may want to ask for volunteers to serve on a Curriculum Review Committee, which will analyze pertinent information and make periodic reports to the faculty. This committee would be responsible for reaching consensus on the schoolwide curriculum and for recommending changes. The entire faculty would then discuss the committee findings and recommendations and approve any specific actions that would affect their classrooms. Like the committee, the faculty must assume responsibility for arriving at a group consensus and for initiating recommended changes.

Whenever possible, it is preferable that all schools within a district undertake this process and that it begin with the appointment of a districtwide curriculum committee comprised of representatives from each school, from the district office, from the school board, and from parent and community groups. Ideally, such a group would study and debate critical issues that affect all educators in the district, such as assessment measures, reporting devices, and adoption of textbooks.

The first step in any planning effort is to assess current strengths and needs with respect to the desired changes. When the goal is to create a whole language program, a needs assessment can help the faculty identify where they are and what they need in order to continue moving toward this goal. The information gained from the instruments discussed earlier in this chapter would help the group determine how many and which teachers need more information about basic beliefs and practices involved in whole language. Additionally, surveys such as the one shown in Figure 3.1 could be constructed by members of the committee to help them gather information about the perceived needs of each teacher.

A helpful observation guide for supervisors and administrators who work with teachers in transition was developed by MaryEllen Vogt (1991). In her article she states that the list of questions that comprise the observation guide was derived from "current research and practice (California State Department of Education, 1987; Cullinan, 1987; Goodman, 1986; Macon, Bewell, & Vogt, 1989; Vogt, 1989)" (p. 209). She further states that the questions included as a part of the guide "presume a degree of acceptance of the whole language philosophy as well as a basic understanding of integrated teaching methods" (p. 209) and that the questions, although divided into the categories of reading, writing, listening, speaking, and general, are interrelated processes that should occur simultaneously. Questions include: "In this classroom, is the teacher modeling and teaching the stages of the writing process (prewriting, drafting, sharing, revising, editing, publishing)?" and "In this classroom, is the teacher teaching students to facilitate group discussion?" (p. 208). Vogt suggests that teachers, administrators, and supervisors first discuss the questions on the observation guide and then allow time for the teachers to become comfortable with some of the strategies before administrators use the guide as an observation tool. She further suggests that teachers and administrators meet before an observation period to agree on which elements will be evaluated during the administrator's

Figure 3.1

SCHOOL STAFF SURVEY

Dear Colleagues,

   The Curriculum Committee has been charged with the task of recommending a plan for staff development for the coming year. To help us focus our efforts, please indicate your level of experience with the following whole language strategies: (Check all that apply.)

   1. *Use of real literature for teaching reading through activities such as: reading workshops, literature-study groups, shared and guided reading strategies.*

   _____ I have had no practical experience teaching reading with these whole language strategies.

   _____ I have incorporated some literature into my reading program but would like to make more use of these strategies.

   _____ I would like to participate in inservice activities that focus on the use of these strategies.

   _____ I feel very confident in my ability to use these whole language strategies for teaching reading.

   _____ I would be willing to share my expertise in this area with others.

   2. Use of a process approach for teaching writing.

   _____ While I am familiar with this term, I have had no practical experience with this whole language strategy.

   _____ I have incorporated some use of the writing process into my classroom, but would like to more fully implement a process writing approach.

   _____ I would like to participate in inservice activities that focus on the implementation of a process writing approach.

   _____ I feel very comfortable with my implementation of a process approach for writing.

   _____ I would be willing to share my expertise in this area with others.

   3. Use of thematic units incorporating as many curricular areas as possible.

   _____ While I have heard of this idea, I have had no practical experience with thematic unit planning/delivery.

   _____ I have tried one or two thematic units and would like to plan and implement more themes.

   _____ I would be interested in participating in inservice activities pertaining to thematic unit planning/delivery.

   _____ I feel very comfortable with using this approach for teaching and learning.

   _____ I would be willing to share my expertise in this area with others.

visit to the classroom.

Gail Heald-Taylor (1989) has developed instruments for assessing a whole language school and for determining teachers' progress toward implementing a whole language program. In her *Whole Language School Assessment Inventory,* teachers and administrators rate as ineffective, somewhat effective, effective, or very effective various components of their program according to a number of criteria listed under the headings: Listening, Speaking, Reading, Writing, Interpretive Activities, and Evaluation. For example, under the heading Reading is the question "How effective is your whole language program in providing student opportunities for reading a variety of genre (fact, fiction, poetry, narrative, biography, etc.)?" Similarly, Heald-Taylor's *Whole Language Progress Indicator* allows for ratings of once a day or more, twice weekly, weekly, twice monthly, and monthly or less for a variety of indicators divided into the areas of Literature, Speaking, Writing, Interpretive Activities, and Evaluation. Specific indicators include such statements as "Students read fiction and nonfiction," "Students are involved in novel studies," and "Students are involved in author studies."

After the teachers respond to the questions on instruments such as the ones discussed above, the Curriculum Committee tallies the responses and uses this information to make recommendations concerning the areas that need to be addressed first in the district or school action plan. The information would also yield important insights into staff development activities, purchase of resources, and so forth.

An alternative to the paper-and-pencil type surveys could be a brainstorming session in which the faculty were encouraged to respond to open-ended questions similar to some of those on the sample instruments. If the staff is large, it could divide into either mixed groups or grade-level groups. Each group would record its answers to the questions on large sheets of chart paper. The group leader or facilitator would then ask each group to read its responses aloud. At the same time a member of each of the other groups would check off duplicate responses on her or his group's chart. Each succeeding group would share only those responses that differ from ones previously mentioned. A chart reflecting a cumulative list of responses would thus be constructed. The groups would then rank in order of importance each item on the cumulative list, with the object of reaching consensus on which needs should be addressed first. For example, if ten out of fifteen teachers felt that "implementation of process writing" was the first priority, followed by "use of children's literature" and "thematic unit planning," these three needs would become the first objectives addressed in the action plan. Another alternative could be to circulate an open-ended questionnaire among all staff members. Each person would respond to each question after reading others' responses. The questionnaire would keep circulating until everyone had read the responses of others in the group and had the chance to change their own responses, if they wanted. After the questionnaire had circulated about three or four times, a meeting would be held to discuss any inconsistencies. This information would then be used in writing the action plan.

Figure 3.2 depicts a possible format for a school and/or district plan. The faculty and staff of each school, through a curriculum committee, would be involved in the development of a schoolwide improvement plan that complemented the district plan for curriculum improvement.

Effective Staff Development. Erickson (1990) cites as effective administrators those who work collaboratively with teachers, parents, and children to plan and implement needed changes. Inherent in this description is the assumption that some form of staff development or inservice education will occur. While we have emphasized the critical role of the teacher in assuming responsibility for staff development, at the same time we realize that not all teachers will be ready to accept this responsibility. Only after a teacher has received sufficient information about a whole language philosophy and compatible educational methodology will she or he be inclined to implement, even on a trial basis, new ways of living and learning in the classroom. Even as teachers come to "own" a whole language philosophy they will often need and want information and help in making the transition from a traditional, subskills, transmission model of education to a transactional whole language model. Thus effective staff development activities are essential.

A NOTE FROM KATHY...

As a university professor I am frequently called upon to conduct inservice training for neighboring school districts. Through the years I have presented numerous "one-shot" presentations—sessions designed to provide something for everyone in less than two hours, with no provision for follow-up. Although I do a nice "song and dance," if I do say so myself, in order to promote substantial, lasting changes, I have begun to work only with those schools and districts that are working toward implementing a long-term plan of action. My involvement with the teachers and administrators in these systems, although more challenging, demanding, and time-consuming, is infinitely more rewarding.

Although there is a wealth of information about effective staff

Figure 3.2

SCHOOL/DISTRICT ACTION PLAN

1. *Formulating a goal.* This is a statement of broad intent, purpose, or direction. It is general and timeless and is not concerned with a particular task to be performed within a specified time.

EXAMPLES:

(District) Provide the students of the district with a curriculum aimed at producing self-motivated, active learners and problem solvers who possess the knowledge, skills, and attitudes necessary for surviving as life-long learners and citizens in the Twenty-first Century.

(School) Provide the students of our school with a developmentally appropriate curriculum that integrates instruction in the content areas with instruction in listening, speaking, reading, writing, and problem solving and that fosters independence through collaborative learning and peer-teaching strategies.

2. *Writing specific objectives.* These are clear statements of measurable objectives. They are derived from the goal and when completed should increase the probability that the goal will be reached. Each objective should answer the following questions:

    1. WHAT is to be done?

    2. WHO will do it?

    3. WHEN is it to be accomplished?

EXAMPLES:

(District) The curriculum committee will assess the needs and desires of principals, teachers, and other school personnel with respect to staff development opportunities, curricular materials, and other means of support.

(School) The curriculum committee will assess teacher needs and desires with respect to staff development opportunities, curricular materials, and other means of support.

3. *Action Plan.* This defines the step-by-step process necessary to achieve a particular objective. The Action Plan usually includes:

  a. Activities aimed at:

    1. accomplishing the objective(s)

    2. providing inservice training for various groups

    3. monitoring and supervising progress toward each objective

    b. person(s) responsible for completing each activity

    c. materials needed

    d. estimated time required to complete each activity, which establishes a beginning and completion date

    e. cost

    f. expected outcomes: the desired result of each proposed activity

    g. documentation: how the completion of each activity will be recorded

    h. evaluation: a careful critique of each action step as it relates to the achievement of the specific objective and to the accomplishment of the overall goal.

development (Fullan, 1990; Paulu, 1989; Vacca, 1981, 1989; Orlich, 1989; Siedow, 1985; Joyce & Showers, 1980; McLaughlin & Berman, 1977), most of us are all too familiar with the "dial-an-inservice" type of staff development that has, unfortunately, characterized too many of these offerings. To be truly effective, staff development activities must be an integral part of the overall action plan. Further, the teachers must be actively involved in making decisions about content, method of delivery, and selection of staff development leaders, speakers, or facilitators. Ideally, these decisions would be made by the entire faculty, based on recommendations from either the curriculum committee or a staff development subcommittee. In developing their recommendations, the group charged with this responsibility would refer to the action plan that was developed and adopted by the entire faculty. This plan would guide the topic choices, follow-up activities, and time frame.

When left to their own devices most teachers have no difficulty sharing their preferences in methods of staff development. Teachers, having been subjected to a wide variety of inservice presentations and staff development offerings, have developed a pretty keen eye for the value of a particular presentation or activity in meeting their needs, interests, and preferences. Most teachers prefer presenters who are able to share information in an enthusiastic, knowledgeable, and organized manner. Additionally, they like to see rather than simply hear about new strategies; therefore, concrete examples, demonstrations, and so forth are generally favored over a strict "lecture" approach. According to Moss (1992), in her article about effective whole language staff development programs, the principles of good instruction should be represented in all staff development offerings. These are, as stated by Moss: "1) linking new information to the known; 2) presenting information in ways consistent with program objectives and whole language practice; 3) allowing teachers to practice new learning in a non-threatening situation" (p. 302).

In terms of staff development, the old adage "To each his own" certainly seems to hold true. Some individuals and groups prefer to be actively involved in discussions and small group activities. Others prefer to sit back, listen, and let the information "gel" for awhile before they enter into a discussion or demonstration. Some individuals prefer to meet at their "home school" while others prefer to meet in new surroundings; some prefer to work for periods as long as a whole day or several days while others prefer shorter periods of time, such as a half-day or even an hour or so after school. Since it is impossible to meet everyone's needs at the same time, it is important to offer variety in the presentation, delivery, times, and locations of staff development activities. One system tried to accommodate teachers' various needs by scheduling two half-day sessions and two full-day sessions. The full-day sessions were held in the community room of the local shopping mall, and the teachers really enjoyed the chance to have lunch or to go shopping together during the noon hour. Recognizing that not all teachers have the same needs and interests at the same time, the district leaders issued invitations rather than requests that teachers attend these staff development offerings. The teachers were to select a certain number of hours of inservice education from a variety of offerings held throughout the school year. Critical information about the district action plan was presented in various ways in a number of different staff development offerings.

If the services of one or more outside consultants are to be secured, members of the committee will probably want to arrange for meetings with them to share the philosophy, action plan, and needs to be addressed. If "hands-on" involvement of the participants is desired, the consultant needs to know this. If large-group meetings for the purpose of sharing information are the primary goal, then that message needs to be conveyed to the consultant. Whatever the desired means of presentation and delivery, there must be clear communication between the outside consultant and the members of the planning committee. Recently, a teacher in a neighboring school system described a particular after-school inservice session. (Admittedly, after school is generally not the best time for staff development activities; however, it seems to be when many such offerings take place.) Naturally, the teachers were tired after a long day; however, they were looking forward to being mentally stimulated by the visiting consultant's presentation. After a fifteen-minute overview of whole language, the consultant asked the teachers to divide into groups to plan and try out several different teaching strategies. Reluctantly, the teachers complied and spent the next hour working in groups. This was more mental stimulation than they bargained for at 3:30 in the afternoon! What they thought was going to be a lively lecture/discussion turned out to be a challenging and even overwhelming exercise for some of the teachers. Fortunately, the teachers did not "blame" the consultant for her method of presentation; rather, they realized that their failure to communicate their needs had resulted in a mismatch of purposes. The consultant's purpose was to involve teachers in hands-on learning experiences while the members of the group had a different purpose—to gain important background information that would motivate them to seek out new strategies.

A SUGGESTED STAFF DEVELOPMENT PLAN.

Although the list of topics in any staff development plan would vary from system to system and perhaps from school to school, in this section we propose topics that generally would be addressed at one time or another by most schools and districts that are moving toward a program based on a whole language philosophy of education. Each system and school would need to evaluate the need for each topic and to ensure maximum teacher input into decisions about subsequent staff development offerings.

Topics

I. Basic Tenets of a Whole Language Philosophy

II. Implementing a Whole Language Philosophy: What's "Wholey" and What's Not!

III. Reading as a Constructive Process: Theory and Application
    A. Emergent Literacy Stage
        1. Stages of Writing Development
        2. Contrasting Traditional "Reading Readiness" with the Concept of Emergent Literacy
        3. Developing Important Concepts about Print
        4. Early Detection of Reading Difficulties
    B. Reading as a Strategic, Meaning-getting Process
        1. Contrasting a Traditional, Reproductive View of Reading with a Constructive One
        2. The Role of the Reader in Assessing and Using Prior Knowledge in Building Comprehension
        3. The Role of the Reader in Applying Strategies for Active Processing of Text
        4. Strategies for Fostering Reading as a Strategic, Meaning-getting Process
            (a) Reciprocal Teaching: Predicting, Summarizing, Clarifying, and Questioning (Palinscar & Brown)
            (b) Question-Answer Relationships (Raphael)
            (c) The Directed-Reading-Thinking Activity (Stauffer)
            (d) KWL: What I Know, What I Want to Know, What I Learned
    C. A Balanced Decoding Program
        1. The Role of Phonics
        2. The Three Cue Systems: Phonology, Syntax, and Semantics
        3. Skills vs. Strategies
        4. Inductive vs. Deductive Instruction

IV. Whole Language Strategies
    A. Using REAL Literature in the Reading Program
        1. Use of Literature during the Emergent and Beginning Reading Stages
            (a) Shared Reading: Charts, Songs, Chants, Rhymes, Poems
            (b) Predictable Literature
            (c) Big Books
            (d) Guided Reading
         2. Selecting and Using Trade Books in the Elementary and Middle School Reading Program

   (a) Implementing Literature-Study Groups
   (b) Organizing for Readers Workshop and Minilessons
   (c) Strategies for Cooperative Group Learning
   (d) Engaging Students in Reciprocal Teaching: Predicting, Questioning, Clarifying, and Summarizing
   (e) Engaging Students in Various Responses to Literature
  B. Implementing a Process Writing Approach
   1. Strategies for Prewriting and Drafting
   2. The Author's Chair
   3. Revision Strategies
   4. The Editing Stage: Strategies for Dealing with the Mechanics of Spelling, Handwriting, Grammar, and Punctuation
   5. Publishing Options
  C. Writing to Learn and as a Response to Reading
   1. The Reading-Writing Connection: Theory and Application
    (a) Journal Writing
    (b) Learning Logs
   2. Writing across the Curriculum
  D. Thematic Unit Planning and Delivery
   1. Criteria for Theme Selection
   2. Themestorming: Planning the Unit
   3. Integrating the Language Processes with Content Area Material
   4. Culminating Activities
 V. Strategies for Kid-watching: Assessing, Evaluating, and Reporting Pupil Progress
  A. Observation Strategies
  B. Creating and Using Anecdotal Records
  C. Creating and Using Checklists
  D. Analyzing Writing Samples
  E. Assessing Oral Reading Performance
  F. Developing and Using a Portfolio Assessment System
 VI. Building Positive Home-School-Community Relationships

ON THE ROAD TO CHANGE.

  Like most long journeys, the move toward whole language requires quite a bit of planning and preparation. Just as there are many routes to any destination, there are many roads to whole language. And as with most journeys, the roads are not all straight and smooth. Developing a whole language program is often a bumpy process, particularly in the initial stages when long-held beliefs and practices are being challenged and new ways of living and learning in the classroom are being explored. There may be a great temptation to shortchange this process, to forge ahead by mandating change. But, as Blum and Kneidek point out, "[I]n the rush to improve, it is much easier to just move ahead, thinking that people will come along. They won't. Districts involved in strategic improvement should be prepared to spend time and effort on the task" (1991, p. 21).

A POSTSCRIPT FROM KATHY...

A central theme of this chapter has been the role of the administrator in supporting teacher change efforts. While we have not singled out the role of the district superintendent, it is certainly one of great importance.

In closing, I want to share with you a few comments of Charles Waggoner, superintendent of one of our neighboring school districts. He enrolled in my graduate early childhood reading methods course to learn more about the teaching of reading during the preschool and primary years. In-depth exposure to a whole language philosophy and the implementation of a whole language program prompted some fairly significant changes in his beliefs about reading. In one paper, he wrote: Master teachers have always "extended" the lesson beyond the text or story. I do find, however, that once the teachers become aware of what they are doing, that they find new and interesting ways to do it. At one time I viewed a class play of Little Red Riding Hood, for example, as just a diversion. Now I see it as literature extension. As Joel A. Barker would say, my "paradigm" has changed.

References:

– **Areglado, N. H., & Stevick, L.** (1991). Suggestions for organizing a whole language networking group. In *The whole language catalog*. American School Publishers, Macmillan/McGraw Hill.

– **Barclay, K.** (1991). Primary teachers involved in change: A special kind of learning. *Reading Horizons, 32(1),* 53–62.

– **Blum, R. E., & Kneidek, A. W.** (1991). Strategic improvement that focuses on student achievement. *Educational Leadership, 48(7),* 17–21.

– **California State Department of Education.** (1987). *The English-language arts framework.* Sacramento, CA: Author.

– **Carnine, D.** (1988). How to overcome barriers to student achievement. In S. J. Samuels and P. D. Pearson (Eds.), *Changing school reading programs* (pp. 59–94). Newark, DE: International Reading Association.

– **Christ, R. A., & Nettles, D. H.** (1992). On the road to whole language: How far have you traveled? *Teaching pre k-8, 22(8),* 66–67.

– **Cullinan, B.** (Ed.). (1987). *Children's literature in the reading program.* Newark, DE: International Reading Association.

– **Datta, L. E.** (1980). Changing times: The study of federal programs supporting educational change and the case for local problem solving. *Teachers College Record, 82,* 101–115.

– **Deal, T. E.** (1990). Reframing reform. *Educational Leadership, 47(8),* 6–12.

– **DeFord, D. E.** (1987). Validating the construct of theoretical orientation in reading instruction. *Reading Research Quarterly, 20(3),* 351–367.

– **Erickson, L. G.** (1990). How improvement teams facilitate schoolwide reading reform. *Journal of Reading, 33,* 580–585.

– **Fullan, M. G., & Miles, M. B.** (1992). Getting reform right: what works and what doesn't. *Phi Delta Kappan, 73(10),* 745–752.

– **Fullan, M. G.** (1990). Staff development, innovation, and institutional development. In B. Joyce (Ed.), *Changing school culture through staff development* (pp. 3–25). Alexandria, VA: Association for Supervision and Curriculum Development.

– **Fullan, M. G., Bennett, B., & Rolheiser-Bennett, C.** (1990).Linking classroom and school improvement. *Educational Leadership, 47(8),* 6–12.

– **Gallagher, M. C., Goudvis, A., & Pearson, P. D.** (1988). Principles of organizational change. In

S. J. Samuels and P. D. Pearson (Eds.), *Changing school reading programs,* (pp. 11–40). Newark, DE: International Reading Association, 1988.

– **Goodman, K.** (1986). *What's whole in whole language?* Portsmouth, NH: Heinemann.

– **Goodman, K., Bird, L., & Goodman, Y.** (1991). *The whole language catalog.* American School Publishers, Macmillan/McGraw-Hill.

– **Goodman, K., Bird, L., & Goodman, Y.** (1991). What is whole language? In *The whole language catalog* (p. 4). American School Publishers, Macmillan/McGraw-Hill.

– **Goodman, K.** (1991). A letter to teachers new to whole language. In *The whole language catalog* (p. 10). American School Publishers, Macmillan/McGraw-Hill.

– **Hall, G., Loucks, S., Rutherford, W., & Newlove, B.** (1975). Levels of use of an innovation: A framework for analyzing innovation adoption. *The Journal of Teacher Education, 34,* 226–233.

– **Heald-Taylor, G.** (1989). *The administrator's guide to whole language* (pp. 62–73). Katonah, NY: Richard C. Owen.

– **Hentel, L.** (1991). How to start your own grass-roots whole language organization. In *The whole language catalog* (p. 412). American School Publishers, Macmillan/McGraw-Hill.

– **Illinois Association for Supervision and Curriculum Development Think Tanks.** (1991). *A report of the IASCD Think Tank.* Normal, IL: Illinois State University.

– **Joyce, B., & Showers, B.** (1980). Improving inservice training: The messages of research. *Educational Leadership, 39,* 379–385.

– **Kuhn, T. S.** (1970). *The structure of scientific revolutions.* Chicago: University of Chicago Press.

– **Lieberman, A., & McLaughlin, M. W.** (1992). Networks for educational change: Powerful and problematic. *Phi Delta Kappan, 73(9),* 673–677.

– **McLaughlin, M., & Berlin, P.** (1977). Retooling staff development in a period of retrenchment. *Educational Leadership, 35,* 191–194.

– **Macon, J., Bewell, D., & Vogt, M. E.** (1989). *Responses to literature: K-8.* Newark, DE: International Reading Association.

– **Meyer, L.** (1988). Research on implementation: What seems to work. In S. J. Samuels and P. D Pearson (Eds.), *Changing school reading programs* (pp. 41–58). Newark, DE: International Reading Association.

– **Moss, B.** (1992). Planning effective whole language staff development programs: A guide for staff developers. *Reading Horizons, 32(4),* 299–315.

– **Orlich, D. C.** (1989). *Staff development: Enhancing human potential.* Boston: Allyn & Bacon.

– **Paulu, N.** (1989). Principals and school improvement: Sixteen success stories. *NAASP Bulletin, 73(517),* 71–77.

– **Peterson, R., and Eeds, M.** (1990). *Grand conversations.* New York: Scholastic.

– **Siedow, M. D.** (1985). Inservice education for content area teachers: Some basic principles. In M. D. Siedow, D. M. Memory, & P. S. Bristow (Eds.), *Inservice education for content area teachers* (pp. 1–7). Newark, DE: International Reading Association.

– **Vacca, J. L.** (1981). *Establishing criteria for staff development personnel* (Contract No. 400–79–0053). Washington, DC: National Institute of Education.

– **Vacca, J. L.** (1989). Staff development. In S. B. Wepner, J. Feeley, & D. Strickland, (Eds.), *The administration and supervision of reading programs* (pp. 93–106). New York: Teachers College Press.

– **Vogt, M. E.** (1991). An observation guide for supervisors and administrators: Moving toward integrated reading/language arts instruction. *The Reading Teacher, 45(3),* 206–211.

– **Vogt, M. E.** (1989). Toward literature-based reading instruction in California. *Reading Today. 6(3),* 19, 580–585.

A Day in a Whole Language Classroom

A NOTE FROM ELIZABETH . . .

We welcome visitors into our building, and I enjoy conducting tours of the classrooms in our school. I frequently find myself trying to see each classroom through the eyes of visitors, wanting to know what they see that piques their interest, that makes them want to take a closer look. As we enter one classroom we see the teacher seated at a table with a small group of children who are sharing their writing with one another. The teacher is listening attentively as the children offer helpful comments and suggestions to the "author" who just read her piece to the group. But this is not what intrigues today's visitor. It is what the other children in the room are doing that makes this visitor want to take a closer look. As we look around the room, we see that these children are not seated at desks placed in rows. There are no worksheets on which everyone is silently working. These children are all doing different things. A pair of children are working at the computer. One is typing as the other contributes story ideas and spellings for words used in their story. There are a number of children seated around a giant cartoon that is placed on the floor. They are each working on a section of the cartoon. At another table we see a group of children writing letters to Eric Carle, the author of the book they are reading during their literature study. And in still another area of the room children are gathered around a crate of books. In the crate are all types of books about bugs, and the children are using the books to obtain "bug facts" that they are recording on bubbles placed around an enormous web. All over the room children are working on various tasks. They are working cooperatively and they are helping each other while the teacher devotes her attention to the children who are seated at the table.

Most people visiting a whole language classroom for the first time find it almost unbelievable that so many chidren involved in such many and varied activities as those described above can remain on task. As we discussed in chapter two a whole language classroom is a "community of learners," and a whole language teacher uses classroom management strategies that promote the qualities of a community. This comes naturally to some teachers, but others may find it difficult to relinquish the control that often characterizes traditional classrooms. The administrator lends active support by reassuring teachers of the importance of establishing this climate while understanding that the process takes place gradually. The strategies used depend not only on the preferences of each teacher but also on the personalities of the children in each classroom. But although classroom management strategies vary from teacher to teacher, all whole language classrooms have certain characteristics in common with respect to classroom management. In the section that follows we briefly discuss six shared characteristics. The remainder of the chapter is devoted to taking you, the reader, on a narrated tour through two whole language classrooms at Oakwood School.

Classroom Management Strategies

1. *The rules of the classroom are negotiated by teachers and children.* Knowing that children learn best in a climate of cooperation and participation, teachers immediately begin to foster such a climate. From the first day of a new school year, the teachers and children work jointly to establish classroom rules. A great deal of discussion takes place as these rules are negotiated and recorded. The discussions generally involve conduct that needs to be enforced for maximum productivity, universally agreed-upon consequences for violating the rules, special rewards, time constraints, and general criteria for the various projects that children will work on. Many times the consequences children suggest are more punitive than those the teacher would have set; but there is a certain advantage to letting the children discover for themselves whether or not a consequence is fair. When reminded that a particular consequence would apply to everyone in the class, children usually recommend more appropriate consequences. Because of the time they spend developing these rules, the children begin to feel that they have both control of and responsibility for their lives. They begin to see themselves as contributing members of the classroom community and as individuals who have helped shape the inner workings of that community. As the year progresses, rules are often renegotiated, depending on the needs of the community. Sometimes new rules become necessary. At other times a rule becomes unnecessary because of some change in the classroom or school.

2. *Children are encouraged to express themselves freely.* Freedom of expression is a primary ingredient of a democratic classroom community. Teachers who convey, either through words or actions, that the classroom must be quiet are impeding learning by removing opportunities for children to learn from each other. The purpose of seatwork has traditionally been to keep children quiet; therefore, seatwork activities in non-whole language classrooms typically involve repetitive work that children either already know how to do or are not yet ready to do, or they are completely unnecessary for a learner of any ability.

Whole language classrooms are not chaotic. The sounds that we hear coming from whole language classrooms are the sounds of children who are learning to combine language and thought; children who are negotiating, sharing, mentoring, and learning; children who are engaged in cooperative learning, participatory decision making, and inquiry. These skills are not necessarily foreign to children. Inquiry, for example, is a very natural process. But if it is not promoted and encouraged, it can disappear. If children do not have opportunities to develop these skills they cannot take responsibility for their own learning. They cannot become independent learners.

3. *Children are given choices.* In a traditional classroom children are often denied the opportunity to develop decision-making and time-management skills. When the teacher makes all of the decisions about what will be done as well as when and by whom, children who have not learned how to make good decisions and to use time responsibly continue to be kept from doing so. Teachers must be dedicated to the idea that children need to learn to use and budget their time well. To learn these skills they must be given the opportunity to make mistakes and to learn from those mistakes. Self-evaluation and self-control are major goals in our curriculum. In whole language classrooms the schedule is flexible so that children can learn to use their time wisely as they pursue various long-range projects. They are asked to think about their tastes in literature and authors and to use this awareness to help them make good choices in reading material. They are encouraged to be curious, to think about what interests them, and to research those topics. The children are also involved in making choices about various working relationships. Children will work alone at times; at other times they will work with a partner or with a small group of children who share the same interest. The time constraints are loose, allowing children to work at different rates. Children love this freedom and work very hard to keep it. When they know the rules and expectations, when they are allowed to set some of their own agenda with respect to learning outcomes, when they know that their interests and opinions are important, children learn to make good choices.

4. *Children are encouraged to help other children.* In a whole language classroom there are as many teachers as there are learners. That is to say, every person in the classroom is both a teacher and a learner. Inherent in this concept is an awareness of the task of promoting not only structured cooperative learning situations but also informal, naturally occurring opportunities for children to share their knowledge, skills, and abilities. When children take the role of teacher, they are serving as a mentor for another child or group of children. Through the mentoring process, the "teacher" further internalizes his or her own learning. Thus the old adage "You only really learn something when you have to teach it to someone else" holds true in a whole language classroom.

5. *Children have purposes for their learning.* Just as children are given many opportunities to express themselves so that they can develop language proficiency and thinking skills, and just as they are given choices so that they can learn decision making and time management, so too do they make decisions about their purposes for learning. Writing becomes a purposeful activity when an audience—usually someone other than the teacher—is identified. Writing a persuasive essay takes on purpose when students become involved in writing letters to the editor of the local newspaper to express a need for new playground equipment. Likewise, readers have purpose when they read literature and content-area books for information that they will share with the class. Contriving purposes for learning is unnecessary in a whole language classroom, for the learners are engaged in meaningful activities that relate to their world as they know and experience it in the here and now. This is in sharp contrast to the many, many classrooms where the emphasis is on preparing for the world of "tomorrow." Can we really prepare for a world that is rapidly and dramatically changing right before our eyes? Children in whole language classrooms are engaged in learning for today. The activities they are involved in are purposeful because they relate to the world as these children know it. And because change is an obvious characteristic of this world, the children are, in fact, learning important life skills.

6. *Children contribute to the development of the curriculum.* As discussed in chapter two, children and teacher often collaborate on developing thematic units of study. The children help gather resources, create bulletin board displays and exhibits, plan projects and presentations, and work together to achieve the learning outcomes that they have helped determine for each unit. Additionally, children know that even as the unit evolves they are free to present alternatives, to ask new research questions, to suggest new projects, and to request additional resources. This flexibility is what breathes life into each theme study. It also contributes to the theme cycle approach discussed in chapter two—the natural evolution from one theme study to the next. As children develop confidence in their ability to contribute to curricular planning, their motivation and desire to achieve the learning outcomes increase.

Oakwood's Organizational Plan

Sometimes a sense of community takes longer to develop. Children who have never been given choices or the freedom to express themselves must be taught the responsibilities that accompany these privileges. In a whole language school this task becomes easier each year as children move from one classroom community to another. Similarly, once the teachers have experienced living and working within a classroom community they realize that their goals are much easier to achieve and more rewarding than before. Thus they see a classroom community as something that is worth promoting.

The implementation of a whole language philosophy of learning is not dependent on any one organizational plan. However, because of our commitment to the creation of learning communities we feel that the self-contained classroom is more compatible with our school goals. At Oakwood, we place a great deal of emphasis on making connections between what children need to know and be able to do and how they can best learn these. These connections can only be made when the teachers *really* know the children. Through a self-contained plan for classroom organization at kindergarten through grade five, we provide the time needed to establish these important interpersonal relationships. In fact, when a faculty opening recently occurred in a second-grade classroom at Oakwood, a first-grade teacher chose to continue on with the children she had worked with in first grade. The advantages of a teacher working with the same children for two years in a row were enormous!

Connections are made not only within each classroom but also between and among classrooms. When all three first-grade classes were involved in a theme based on Columbus, each classroom celebrated the landing by pretending to be aboard one of the ships. The children in each classroom "boarded" ships made from enormous cardboard boxes and bearing the names of the Niña, the Pinta, and the Santa María. Then, as the children in the three "ships" sailed down the school hallway, banners displayed proudly, one ship sank. This fact of history became very real to the children as they squeezed the "survivors" of the sunken ship into the other two "ships."

Connections are even made across grade levels. For example, many times primary and intermediate grades work on the same theme in a cross-grade collaboration. Once the fifth- and second-grade classrooms were all involved in a study of weather. The fifth-graders took notes for their own research papers while helping the second-grade children get facts for their reports. The second-grade children were motivated by the attention received from the older students, who took their responsibility very seriously. The cross-grade partners even recorded their information on videotape; this was then shared with the other second- and fifth-grade students and their parents.

Even when children have special classes such as music, art, physical education, and speech, an effort is made to make sure that what happens outside of the classroom connects with what is happening inside. To this end, art and music teachers plan their curricula to complement the themes being studied in each classroom. For example, when the second-grade classes were studying African folktales, the children made African masks in art and sang chants and rhythms in music. Even the teachers in the learning disabilities and speech classes worked to coordinate their activities with those taking place in the regular classroom. These teachers quickly realize how much more motivated the children are when the curricula in these special classrooms complement that in the regular classroom. These special services presently are provided through either a "pull out" resource room plan of organization or through the "class within a class" plan, in which the special teacher goes into the regular classroom to help individual children. Both of these organizational plans have worked well for us because both plans reflect a strong belief in helping all children make connections.

Come into My Classroom . . .

Now that we have explained the six shared characteristics of each teacher's plan for classroom management, we invite you to visit two whole language classrooms. We begin by describing a day in a primary-grade classroom. After discussing the many, many activities going on throughout the day, we move on to an upper-elementary classroom where we again describe the activities taking place over an entire day in a whole language classroom. The classrooms described in this section are typical of classrooms in any of the primary (kindergarten through second) or intermediate (third through fifth) grades.

A Primary-Grade Classroom: A Whole Day of Whole Language

It is 8:15 and the children are just entering the room when we arrive. After being greeted warmly by the teacher, they begin to follow a routine that this teacher knows is an important part of the classroom structure. As they come into the room, the children record on a chart what they want for lunch by writing their name in the appropriate place. The chart also serves as a record of attendance for that day. When they have completed this task, the children give the teacher notes signed by their parents confirming that they had done independent reading the night before.

At approximately 8:30 the children begin to write in their journals. These are dialogue journals that record a written conversation between the teacher and each child. The teacher never fails to respond to what each child has written. These entries give the teacher important insights into each child's life. Further, the journal becomes a means of assessment and enables the teacher to model standard written language based on each child's needs. The journal also serves as a record of each child's growth as a writer, since the entries are dated and the journals are kept in the classroom all year. As the children complete their entries for the day, the teacher moves from child to child, responding to each entry. This process works well because, as this teacher explains, the children at this level benefit most from the immediate feedback that she supplies. While responding to a child's entry is often very easy, sometimes a response requires more time and thought. For example, today the teacher spends time with a child who needs encouragement in writing a one-word description of a picture that he has drawn on the journal page. Because the teacher is using this time to assess student progress, she writes a response to the child about the picture. She makes a note to herself that, when writing the word swimming, the child asked what the letter *m* looked like.

Figures 4.1, 4.2, and 4.3 show three very different journal entries and the teacher's response to each. Figure 4.1 shows Ben's journal entry. He writes, "Life is like climbing a mountain. When you are born you start at the bottom and when you get to the top you pass away." His teacher responds with a very simple yet infinitely appropriate statement: "This is poetry, Ben." Since poetry is very special in this classroom, Ben understands that the teacher is complimenting him on his entry. Figure 4.2 shows Jason's letter to his teacher. He writes, "Dear Mrs. Veatch, I am sorry I've been a pain in the butt. I have been mad. I have took it out on the kids and you. Tomorrow I will be better." Note how the teacher's response invites Jason to tell or write more about his feelings. Figure 4.3 shows Denzil's journal entry. He writes, "I was mad when my Dad took my money and my face was red. Every morning my face is red. Ryan said 'What happened to your face?' 'My Dad took my money. That's the way it happened.' When I got an 'A-' I got my money back and I was happy and my Dad was sorry." In response to Denzil's entry the teacher writes, "Dear

Figure 4.1

BEN'S JOURNAL ENTRY

Life is Like kLim,
a ma whTN weh you
are BorN yr strkt N a
the BoTm and wen you
geT to the Both Top
you Pas awy

This is poetry Ben

By

Bch

Denzil, I am glad you got your money back."

The children in this classroom are used to this routine. They know that they will each have their own special time to share their journal entry with the teacher; therefore, while the teacher is busy with other students in the class, the other students are involved in a variety of activities. They may be reading their journals or adding to a particular entry if the teacher has made a suggestion that motivates them to do so. They may be getting ready for group meeting, particularly if it is their turn to share. There is always a variety of learning centers available, as well as new items to explore at the discovery table. Because both the teacher and each child value the time they spend together, the teacher has structured the environment to minimize distractions and interruptions by promoting children's active involvement in their tasks.

By the time the last journal has been put away it is 9:00—time for group meeting. The children who used some of the preceding time to read or to work

Figure 4.2

JASON'S JOURNAL ENTRY

Mrs. Veatch
I am srow I've been a pan in the
butt I have been mad
I have took it out
on the kids a you tomorrow
I will be butter.

Jason,
Can you tell me what
you've been mad about?
Sometimes it helps to talk
about things that make you
mad. It helps you to feel
better inside.

Figure 4.3

DENZEL'S JOURNAL ENTRY

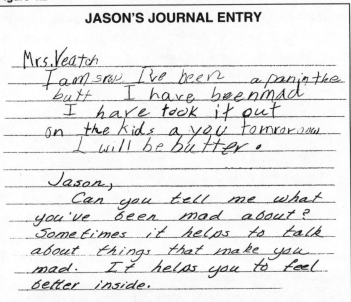

I was mad

When mr dad took
mr mane ant mr
fasse was red evere
morning mr fazzs is
red "Ryon said what happn
to your fose mr Dad
took mr mane thas
the way it happn When
I got a a-o- I got
mr mane backo
And I was happy
Ant mr dad was
sere. Dear Denzil,
I am glad you got your
money back.

at the learning centers return the books and materials to their proper places and join the other children on the rug. The rules for the group meeting, negotiated early in the school year, include taking turns sharing and respecting everyone's individual space. Having to return to your chair is the agreed-upon consequence for violating the group meeting rules.

Teachers use the group meeting to achieve many objectives. To start with, it is a time for oral sharing, when the literacy skills of listening and speaking are both addressed. In this classroom the children take turns sitting in front of the group and sharing. Children who have lost a tooth or have special news about a birth or death in the family share first. In addition, the names of three other children who will take turns sharing are drawn out of a bag that is pinned to the bulletin board. Today, two of the children share personal experiences and Ben shares his exceptional journal entry. The experiences the children describe are rich and varied and contribute to the feeling of community in this classroom.

Number concepts dealing with dates and time are taught as the children participate in activities that are simply called "calendar." During "calendar" teacher and children use words for time-order concepts such as *yesterday, tomorrow, next, after, before, finally, first* and *last*. They also learn the months of the year, days of the week, and seasons of the year and practice counting by ones, twos, fives, and tens. The children also practice telling time. Today, the children count the number of days since they began the current unit of study and the number of days until they go on a theme-related field trip. The teacher asks volunteers to go up to the big wall calendar to point and count, first by ones and then by fives. Other children are asked to read several messages written on the calendar to remind the class about various upcoming events. One new reminder about a school assembly to be held the following week is recorded. The teacher then moves over to the chart stand, which is placed near the front of the rug. It is time for Shared Reading.

During this part of the group meeting, big books and poetry, songs, and chants that have been recorded on large sheets of chart paper are often used. Children at all levels of development benefit from the Shared Reading time, since each child participates at his or her own level. Some children are involved only in the pictures while others can read every word. Some children are developing an understanding of how words and sentences are put together—learning that print has meaning—while others are learning new vocabulary words and new strategies for decoding words and figuring out meaning. Often the content of the material is related to the theme that is currently being studied. For example, today the class reads a book and two poems about space. Beginning with one of the poems, the teacher invites the children to read along with her as she points to each word with a pointer that has a star attached to the end. As the children read, it is obvious that they have enjoyed this piece on previous days. Next, the teacher invites a child to point to the words as the children read the poem again. The children show as much enthusiasm as they did during the first reading, and much more confidence. The teacher then uses Post-it notes to cover several of the words in the poem. She asks the children to think of other words that would make sense. These words are recorded on other Post-it notes, and the children reread the poem using the new words. The teacher asks the children to think about how the meaning of the poem changes with each substitution.

After this discussion, the teacher directs the children's attention to a new poem chart. She asks the children to look at the title. After they work together to read it, she asks them to predict what the author was thinking about or feeling when he wrote the poem. As the children offer their opinions, the teacher records these on a large sheet of chart paper and asks the children to listen for things in the poem that would support their opinions. The teacher then reads the poem with great expression. After a fair amount of discussion, she rereads the poem, asking the children to join in whenever they feel comfortable doing so.

After reading the poem again, the teacher replaces the chart stand with the big book stand—a special stand for holding enlarged versions of children's books. Today the teacher will share a new book with the children, a work of nonfiction chosen because of the contribution it will make to the theme study. Before opening the book, the teacher asks the children to look again at a chart of questions they prepared a few days before. All the questions are about space. Next, the teacher asks the children to read the title of the new book. After trying several times the children read the title correctly and immediately begin to predict which of their questions the book might answer. When the teacher asks them why they think particular information might be included in this book, they give various reasons based on the title and the picture on the book's cover. The teacher asks them to listen for this information as she reads aloud.

The children listen attentively for about ten minutes, pausing to discuss various bits of information in the text. Next they dictate answers to some of the questions they discussed earlier as well as some new information unrelated to their questions. The teacher records this information on a chart titled "What We Learned about Space." The teacher twice asks the children to reread passages in order to clarify what they are dictating. Each passage contains words that the children are able to read, using their growing knowledge of context, phonics, and sentence structure. The time spent on Shared Reading varies; the teacher is not bound by a schedule but keeps the session going as long as the time is productive. After ten minutes or so the teacher ends the Shared Reading time by inviting the children to reread any of the charts or the new big book during the independent reading work period.

The group's final task is to set the agenda for the rest of the morning. They look at the written agenda and accompanying schedule, noting the time of each activity, and reviewing what the clock will look like at each time. The written agenda is present even when some children in the group cannot read all of it, for whole language classrooms are "print-rich" places where children are constantly exposed to meaningful text.

The teacher notes that it is almost 10:00, time for the first activity on the schedule—Literature Study. Today each group will have thirty minutes with the teacher, one group meeting now and the other two after the morning recess. The literature groups are named by the title of the book they are currently discussing. After the teacher announces the time that each group will meet she asks the children to review what the rest of the class needs to do while the teacher is "at group." Both the routine and the rules are very specific. The children name a number of tasks, including completing journal entries, reading, working at the computer, working on projects, or making entries in their literature logs.

There is a great deal of choice built into this period—choice accompanied by the responsibility to participate in certain types of tasks, such as those related to the children's literature study groups. There are also several learning centers available to children who have completed all of their other responsibilities. Today the teacher has set out a crate of books that will be used to study the next theme. The children can browse through the books, thinking about what they want to investigate for their next research project.

As the children position themselves at the various work sites, one group of five children, literature study books in hand, heads for the table to work with the teacher. On Monday they listened and followed along as the teacher read part of the book to the group. On Tuesday the children read on their own or with the teacher. Since today is Wednesday, they know that they are going to read their favorite parts of the book and discuss entries in their literature logs. Thursday and Friday they will share plans for and work on a project that will demonstrate their understanding and appreciation of the book. These projects take many forms—book covers, cartoon strips, puppet shows, plays, new endings for the story, and so on. The possibilities are endless, and these children generally have no difficulty whatsoever in coming up with new projects for each book. Each member of the literature study group must think about what needs to be done and then do it. Assuming responsibility for these tasks becomes easier as children become accustomed to the routine and to the criteria used to evaluate each task. In the appropriate circumstances even these very young children are able to accept responsibility for working productively, cooperatively, and independently.

As we look around this classroom, what we observe is very similar to the scene described at the beginning of the chapter. The children are actively engaged in a variety of activities. As they move from task to task they know that they are responsible for doing what needs to be done. Several children are planning projects for their literature study group. Some children are writing entries in their literature logs. Three children are looking at the books in the crate and discussing what they already know about the upcoming theme—the ocean. One child says that he wants to know if scientists are going to build "ocean cities" similar to the "space ports" of the future that they learned about in their current theme study. Two children are using the computer as a word processor to type in their version of the first poem shared during the morning group meeting. One child is rereading the big book that was shared during that same meeting.

At 11:30 the teacher has the children look at the schedule and asks them to put away their materials and to get ready for lunch. After lunch the routine continues. First, the children gather on the rug for a group meeting, which opens today with the teacher reading aloud from Marilyn Sadler's *Alistair in Outer Space*. The teacher knows that nothing promotes reading or community like sharing a good book. This particular book was brought from home by one of the children because it relates to the theme that they are studying. After the book sharing, the children discuss the afternoon schedule. Today the afternoon schedule includes a physical education class (see figure 4.4).

During the afternoon, some children leave the room to meet with "special" ed teachers to work on learning and speech disabilities or the Chapter I programs. These interruptions are not disruptive, however, since the class rarely works as a large group.

After the group meeting the children focus on math. While the teacher may use manipulatives to introduce some concepts to the entire class, the children spend most of their time working at the math centers that are set up around the room. As we move from center to center we see dishpans filled

Figure 4.4

AFTERNOON SCHEDULE

12:15 – 12:45	Oral Reading/Group Meeting
12:45 – 1:30	Math
1:30 – 2:00	Physical Education
2:00 – 2:30	Authors' Circle
2:30 – 3:10	Theme Study
3:10 – 3:15	Closure

with various objects—buttons, keys, beads, unifix cubes, blocks, and so forth. There is a limit on the number of children who may work together at any one center, and tasks are designed to accommodate the abilities of each child. This setup allows the teacher to concentrate on individual children or small groups who are working on a particular skill or task. The teacher may use this time to assess children's abilities, to conduct minilessons, and/or to observe children working and take notes on their progress.

Today we are able to watch the teacher work with a group of four children. Each child has a small plastic cup containing ten beans. The beans have been painted white on one side and black on the other. The teacher demonstrates how to spill the beans, count the beans of each color, and record the information on individual charts. After making sure that the children can continue the task without her, she moves on to one of the centers to check on the children's progress. After a few minutes we see her pause to make a note in her assessment notebook. When we inquire about the note later, she explains that the children were working on a patterning activity and one child had, for the first time, accurately designed and recorded his own pattern from the unifix cubes. She had paused to jot down a note about his progress in her assessment notebook.

After visiting another center and "eyeing" the children working at the others, the teacher returns to the children who are counting and recording the beans. She asks them to look at their charts to see if they can make any observations. As they discuss their charts, they begin to comment about how often a particular number of black or white beans turned up. This leads to a discussion of predictability and odds. Before leaving the group, the teacher challenges the children to keep testing their assumptions.

This routine is followed until almost 1:30, when the teacher again has children look at the clock and asks them to put away the math materials. Before the class leaves for P.E., the teacher calls out the names of the students who are scheduled to work in the authors' circle. Each of the students has selected a "space noun" to research, so they are writing reports about planets, spaceships, and so on. She reminds them to bring their notes and their rough drafts with them to the table.

After returning from their P.E. class, the children work on their reports. The children in one group bring to the authors' circle their notes and the first drafts of their space reports. The rest of the children begin to work on their notes and reports. Some children are finding the information they need in books in the classroom. Others are working with partners to correct spelling errors, and still others are working on visuals that will accompany their reports (see figure 4.5). Three fifth-grade students are taking dictation from some first-grade students, and some first-grade students are serving as scribes for other first-graders who need help recording information for their reports.

Children in the authors' circle are sharing their rough drafts. As each child reads her or his draft, the children listen carefully to see whether it makes sense. The teacher expects the listeners to assess both the quality and quantity of each draft. After each report, the teacher asks whether the writer has included good information and whether there is enough of it. Figure 4.6 shows Diane's notes for her report about the planet Mars. It is important that children at all levels know that one doesn't write a report by copying information directly from a book; therefore, these second-grade pupils take notes in list format and then write a rough draft of their report (see figure 4.7).

When all of the children in the group have shared their work and understand their editing and/or revising tasks, the teacher calls the next group of children to the table. As in all classrooms with very young children, these conferences, which are held at least every other day, give the children direct contact with the teacher.

Near the end of the day the children are asked to put away their materials. They file their notes and drafts in a box labeled "Reports," return other supplies to the storage tubs, and then gather on the rug. The teacher quickly reviews the activities that took place during the day and previews the following day. She then asks the children to share one "space fact" as they line up for dismissal. When the bell rings she begins to think about who and what will be on the agenda for the next day.

A Visit to an Intermediate Classroom

Because the teachers in grades three, four, and five are also using

Figure 4.5

*Space

Space is blank,
With a black blank sky,
With billons of stars Twinkling by.
Look out the window look look
Stars billons of stars,
In the black blank sky.

by: Darrell
Mc Cory

Figure 4.6

1. Mars is the 4th planet from the sun.
2. Mars is half the size of Earth.
3. Mars has two moons.
4. Mars often has storms, the dust storms can last for several Earth months
5. Mars has rings around it.
6. You can't run on mars.
7. Nights and days on both planets take about the same time
8. It is red and is a planet.
9. It is made out of soil.
10. Mars has no water.
11. Mars is a litele star in the sky from Earth.
12. Mars is a good place to be.
13. I now why Mars is red soil is red,

from
Diane

NOTES

Figure 4.7

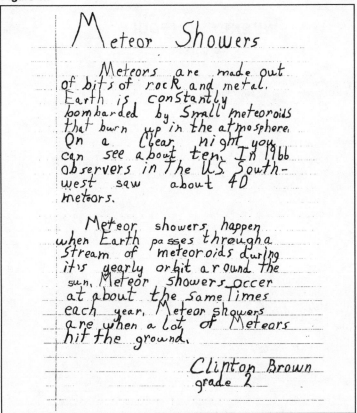

Meteor Showers

Meteors are made out of bits of rock and metal. Earth is constantly bombarded by small meteoroids that burn up in the atmosphere. On a clear night you can see about ten. In 1966 observers in the U.S. Southwest saw about 40 meteors.

Meteor showers happen when Earth passes through a stream of meteoroids during it's yearly orbit around the sun. Meteor showers occer at about the same times each year. Meteor showers are when a lot of Meteors hit the ground.

Clinton Brown
grade 2

classroom management strategies that encourage children to take responsibility for their own learning, these teachers at Oakwood write out daily schedules and give them to the students at the start of each morning (see figure 4.8). During the group meeting, the students will personalize their schedule, highlighting their responsibilities for the day and crossing out completed tasks. At the end of the day, homework assignments are recorded on the bottom of the sheet, which the child takes home. Both teachers and students find that creating these daily schedules helps them better organize their time.

On this particular day, a Monday, the students start the day at 8:25 by writing in their journals. As in the primary-grade classrooms, the journals are used for writing conversations between the teacher and each student. Because of the children's age the entries are usually private, and this teacher generally keeps the journals overnight, returning them with her written responses on the following morning. Again, the teachers view the time spent in reading and responding to each student's journal as valuable, for it gives them a unique opportunity to build a closer relationship with students who

Figure 4.8

WEEKLY SCHEDULE

MONDAY

DATE:

8:25-8:45	Journal		
8:45-9:00	Spelling/Select New Words		
9:00-9:10	Class Meeting		
9:10-9:35	Language Arts	1	_____
		2	_____
		3	_____
9:35-10:30	Science/Social Studies	1	_____
		2	_____
		3	_____
10:30-11:00	Music		
11:00-12:00	Language Arts/Lit Books	1	_____
		2	_____
		3	_____
		4	_____
12:00-12:30	Lunch		
12:30-12:35	Restroom Break		
12:35-1:00	Oral Reading		
1:00-2:00	Math		
2:00-2:25	Recess		
2:25-3:10	Study Time		
3:10-3:15	Class Meeting/Dismiss		

Homework 1 _____
         2 _____
         3 _____

TUESDAY

DATE:

8:25-8:45	Journal		
8:45-8:55	Sustained Silent Reading (S.S.R.)		
8:55-9:00	Class Meeting		
9:00-9:30	P.E.		
9:30-10:00	Music		
10:00-10:30	Science/Social Studies	1	_____
		2	_____
		3	_____
10:30-11:00	Library		
11:00-12:00	Language Arts/Lit Books	1	_____
		2	_____
		3	_____
		4	_____
12:00-12:30	Lunch		
12:30-12:35	Restroom Break		
12:35-1:00	Oral Reading - Book		
1:00-2:00	Math		
2:00-2:25	Recess		
2:25-3:10	Study Hall		
3:10-3:15	Class Meeting/Dismiss		

Homework 1 _____
         2 _____
         3 _____

WEDNESDAY

DATE:

8:25-9:00	P.E.		
9:00-9:30	Spelling Test (Trial)		
9:30-9:35	Class Meeting		
9:35-9:50	S.S.R.		
9:50-10:20	Language Arts	1 _____ 2 _____ 3 _____	
10:20-11:00	Science/Social Studies	1 _____ 2 _____ 3 _____	
11:00-12:00	Language Arts/Lit Books	1 _____ 2 _____ 3 _____ 4 _____	
12:00-12:30	Lunch		
12:30-12:35	Restroom Break		
12:35-1:00	Oral Reading/Book		
1:00-2:00	Math		
2:00-2:25	Recess		
2:25-3:10	Study Hall		
3:10-3:15	Class Meeting		

Homework 1 _____
          2 _____
          3 _____

THURSDAY

DATE:

8:25-8:45	Journal		
8:45-9:00	Newspaper		
9:00-9:30	P.E.		
9:30-10:00	Library		
10:00-11:00	Science/Social Studies	1 _____ 2 _____ 3 _____	
11:00-12:00	Language Arts/Lit Books	1 _____ 2 _____ 3 _____ 4 _____	
12:00-12:30	Lunch		
12:30-12:35	Restroom Break		
12:35-1:00	Oral Reading/Book		
1:00-2:00	Math		
2:00-2:25	Recess		
2:25-3:10	Study Hall		
3:10-3:15	Class Meeting		

Homework 1 _____
          2 _____
          3 _____

are often reluctant to voice their feelings in front of their peers.

The students write in their journals for approximately twenty minutes. Then, since it is Monday, the students know that they are to choose words for their personalized weekly spelling lists. The words on these lists come from group efforts and from individual writing tasks. For example, in the science center this week is an independent study activity dealing with soil and rocks. On the spelling lists are words like *sedimentary* and *igneous*. The students are writing reports about the Westward Movement, so words like *pioneer* and *prairie schooner* appear on many of the lists. In addition, ten of the words on the students' lists are words that they misspelled in their individual writing. After creating their lists, the students have them approved by the teacher. It is then the responsibility of each student to follow the spelling study steps and learn how to spell each word. These study steps are used throughout the grades and are reviewed by each classroom teacher at the start of a new year. On Wednesday there will be a trial test followed by a final test on Friday. Both tests are administered by a spelling partner. While these tests count in the grading scheme, the students' final grades in spelling are derived primarily from the spelling proficiency they demonstrate in their writing.

At 9:00 the students convene for a class meeting. During this time, typically from 9:00 to 9:10, they discuss the schedule, review upcoming deadlines, and settle any problems. If the principal has an issue to discuss with a particular class, this is the best time to do it, since the day's routine would not be interrupted. The class or group meeting is a good time to create a climate of open communication. Often a teacher says to a student, "How about bringing that up at the group meeting?" Today several girls share a list of playground rules that they typed after the previous day's group meeting (see figure 4.9). As the teacher requested, they also share information about why new rules were needed (see figure 4.10). At the close of the meeting, the teacher reminds the students that she will be checking the notecards they have prepared for their research project.

Following the group meeting, the students gather the materials they will need during the independent work period that is about to begin. For approximately the next thirty-five minutes the teacher works with a small group of students who are sharing persuasive essays. The essays will meet a requirement negotiated by the teacher and students at the beginning of the theme on the West. The essays are being compiled in a western newspaper that the students are creating. The newspaper will contain "current" events, advertisements for land and various products, editorials, human interest stories, and political advertisements and endorsements. All of the information in the newspaper will be factual, based on the students' research.

Today Andrea, Jackie, Mark, Erin, and Jason are working on essays on the Homestead Act, the right to fence the range, and the issues of statehood for Kansas. They are working in pairs to read their first drafts to the teacher and the other group members. The information included in their newspaper essays has to be substantiated and referenced, and the children have to make their points of view clear to their listeners and readers. After the partners share each essay, the listeners provide helpful suggestions.

Groups are convened according to the needs and personalities of the pupils. The daily meeting that the teacher holds with different groups of pupils helps her keep track of each student's development as a writer. It also enables her to give minilessons on style, content, and mechanics.

As the students in the authors' circle work on their persuasive essays, the other students work on the current project in their writing folder or on their literature study, research project, or weekly spelling list. All the children have copies of their schedules for the day and know if and when they are scheduled to meet with the teacher and/or with a small group of their classmates.

At 9:35 the authors' circle disbands and the teacher meets with another

Figure 4.9

PLAYGROUND RULES

1. Girls can play games with boys. (Football, basketball, and baseball)
2. Same to girls.
3. Boys should respect girls when they try.
4. Same with girls.
5. Girls have to remember not to tackle – just to touch.
6. With boys too!!!!!!!!!!!
7. When the girls are playing the boys have to ask nicely to play.
8. Same with girls.
9. When going outside NO pushing.
10. No chasing unless both agree.
11. Girls don't put down another player (Like you're no good or you stink.)
12. Same with boys.
13. NO laughing if someone gets hurt.
14. NO laughing is someone misses a play.
15. When playing NO boys against girls – pick mixed teams.
16. Have the same amount of people on a team – if not QUIT.
17. Everybody be fair because it is not fair if you're not.

Figure 4.10

FUNCTIONAL WRITING

This is how we got the idea of the RULES

One day we were at the Super Citizen party and we wanted to play football with the boys but they said NO!! We told the principal that the boys would not let us play. We soon were running down the field but guess what we were not playing we were trying to catch them so they would let us play. We never got to play because the boys kicked us out like we were not even there. The boys said that we could not play because we were not boys. Then Brooke said we were cute little tom boys. We still did not get to play. RaChauna got the ball about 2 inches and then tried to throw it and the boys did not catch it. Brooke then caught the ball. She proved that girls were not too bad after all.

PEOPLE WHO WERE IN IT.

Brooke, Wesley, Austin, Jeremiah, Nathan, Mrs. Boone, Michael, Denise, and RaChauna.

By: Brooke Renberg, RaChauna Adams, and Denise Hurt

small group of students, this time to assess their progress on their research project for the theme under study. Today Mary, John, and Lee meet with the teacher to share their notes for their research project. At the beginning of the theme study, the class set deadlines for each stage of the project. Today the notecards are due. The pupils know that they are to have fifty notes from at least four sources and that the notes are to be color-coded according to categories of information. For example, cards with a red dot might indicate where a particular animal lives. Cards with green dots might have information about what the animal eats. This coding system helps beginning researchers organize their reports into paragraphs.

By establishing "check points" at each stage of the process, both teacher and students ensure the success of the final project. As when the authors' circle was meeting, the other students in the classroom are working on the various tasks described above.

It is 11:00—time for Literature Study. Each day a full hour is set aside for literature study. Because this is a large class, there are usually four literature groups, each group meeting every other day. The teacher meets with two small groups of pupils each day. On the days that the students are not meeting with the teacher to read, discuss, and respond to the book, they are reading the book silently and responding in their literature log to what they have read.

Today the children that are meeting are reading William O. Steele's *The Year of the Bloody Seven* and Joan Blos's *The Gathering of Days,* both of which fit the theme being studied. We notice that boys have chosen to read *The Year of the Bloody Seven,* in which the author depicts aspects of frontier life from the terrain to the guns that people used at the time. The group reading *The Gathering of Days,* the diary of a girl raised in a pioneer home, is comprised entirely of girls. The children chose the books from among several that the teacher "advertised" through book talks.

A group member serves as discussion leader for the thirty-minute session, during which the students read from their literature logs their reactions to the pages they had agreed to read for today. "No wonder the frontier people thought of the Indians as savages. I saw *Dances with Wolves* and felt bad about how we mistreated the Indians, but they are sure mean in this book. I wonder if they are the same Indians" is a reaction shared by one of the boys. Before the group disbands they agree on the number of pages that they will read by the next meeting.

At 12:00 the students put away their books and literature logs and go to lunch. When they return to the classroom at about 12:35, the teacher reads aloud from *Pioneer Women: Voices from Kansas Frontier* by JoAnna Stratton,

Figure 4.11

Student	Notecards	First copy	Revisions	Final copy		Editorials	Ads	News Story	Layout							
1																
2																
3																
4																
5																
6																
7																
8																
9																
10																
11																
12																
13																
14																
15																
16																
17																
18																
19																
20																
21																
22																
23																
24																
25																
26																
27																
28																
29																
30																
31																
32																

Teacher _____ Subject _____ Grade _____ Date _____

a book she chose because of its connection to the theme. A one-hour math block begins at 1:00. During most of this time individuals work in small groups; however, even students in the same group work at their own pace, going from one math concept to the next as they demonstrate mastery of each. As in the primary grades, manipulatives play an important role in the development of mathematical concepts. Additionally, a great deal of math is taught, reinforced, and practiced as a part of the theme being studied. For example, today the teacher poses this question: "How long would a buffalo herd of 10,000 last if 200 buffalo a day were being killed by hunters?"

The children have recess from 2:00 to 2:25. When the students return to the classroom they gather the materials they need for the next forty-five minutes. This is "study time." Knowing what they must have ready for the next day, the students use this time to take care of the things that must be done at school.

A few students ask permission to go to the library for books they need for their research. While they are out of the room, the teacher helps a child use the index in a trade book. Next, the teacher moves around the room, checking on each group's progress on the western newspaper. At the reading table she meets with a group of children who are planning advertisements for the newspaper. As they talk about how much space the advertisements will need, a couple of students go to the office for large sheets of paper on which to lay out the newspaper copy. When they return to the classroom, they begin gluing articles on the paper. Two more computers have been borrowed from other classrooms, and several children are using the word processing programs to create their final drafts.

There is a great deal of activity, but the children are working responsibly and purposefully. They plan to sell these newspapers, so they want the best product possible. Earlier in the year they made and sold baked goods to raise money for the endangered animal they are supporting. During this economics lesson, they learned the frustration of "running out of inventory"—something they do not plan to let happen this time!

While the children are all occupied, the teacher takes a few minutes to begin planning for the next day. She returns to her desk for what the children call "office time." Clipboard in hand, the teacher reviews notes she made during the day and then begins to fill in the blanks of the next day's schedule. She writes down the names of students she needs to see at the authors' circle. She refers to the chart (see figure 4.11) showing the components of the newspaper to see who she has and has not yet met with. She also writes down the deadlines for the various articles and notes who is ready for the word processor.

On the schedule she also records the time that a guest speaker from the *Courier Post* will address the class on how to lay out a newspaper. Next, she writes down the names of the literature study groups and the pages they agreed to read in their books. She also writes notes to three students who have not made checkmarks indicating that they completed their spelling lists. At the bottom of the schedule, the teacher writes her daily trivia question. The question for tomorrow is "Who said, 'Go west, young man'?"

It has been an exceptionally full day. As students return materials to the shelves, we look at the agenda and see that it is time for this classroom's culminating event of the day—a class meeting. This is an event that the teacher tries to work in every day. As she did during the morning meeting, the teacher reminds the class of upcoming deadlines. She also quickly reviews their responsibilities for the next day. Children who still have unfinished work are reminded to make a notation on the bottom of their schedules and to take the work home to complete.

The teacher then asks the students to think about the day's work. Today she asks, "How do you feel about the newspaper? Do you feel that it is going to be saleable? If not, what can we do to make it more attractive to the readers?" These questions prompt both thought and discussion among the students. Though this closing discussion is not long, it is an important part of this day. It serves a valuable role in maintaining the feeling of community shared by these learners.

In Summary

While these two classrooms are typical of the whole language classrooms at Oakwood School, they do not by any means reflect the practices implemented in all whole language classrooms. We cannot emphasize strongly enough *that there is no one way to do whole language.* We described events in these two classrooms merely to provide a "window" through which you might observe whole language in action in one particular school. Now we ask you to reflect again on the shared characteristics of whole language classrooms. That is, while whole language classrooms vary greatly in practice, their common beliefs unite the teachers in those classrooms.

In the two classrooms described in this chapter, as well as in whole language classrooms everywhere, the teachers establish communities of learners. They do this by negotiating classroom rules with the children and by encouraging free expression, peer tutoring, and independent thinking and decision making. Further, the children in whole language classrooms set purposes for their learning and contribute to the development of the curriculum. The children in these classrooms spend time each day in independent reading and writing and in projects and/or research related to a meaningful unit of study. Curriculum is integrated, and the skills of language, literacy, and math are learned as they are *used* to accomplish varied, purposeful tasks. Evaluation is ongoing and continuous, reflecting a strong emphasis on self-evaluation and teacher observation and assessment of both process and product.

As whole schools and individual classrooms move toward a whole language philosophy, teachers and administrators must consider classroom management, time management, organization, curriculum and methodology, and evaluation in light of a strong commitment to the beliefs that unite whole language educators across the globe. While it may be useful to know the specific strategies used in various classrooms and schools, each whole language teacher must tailor his or her own program according to: (1) the characteristics of the learners in that classroom and (2) her or his knowledge and beliefs about how learning best occurs. Understanding the management strategies described in this chapter will help many teachers create and sustain the rich learning communities that are characteristic of whole language classrooms and schools.

A Three-Way Partnership: Linking Home, School, and Community

"New Method Spells Discontent" is the title of an article published in May 1992 by the *Journal Star,* a Peoria, Illinois, newspaper. In the article, journalist Clare Howard reports an incident that happened at a local elementary school where invented spelling is encouraged at the lower-elementary levels. An irate parent is quoted as saying, "It's abominable. I'm astounded teachers aren't stricter. I know I'm in the majority when I say this is ludicrous." Fortunately, Howard interviewed the district assistant superintendent, who was quoted as saying, "It's phenomenal how much better they write, and we have found no breakdown in spelling at the second, third, or fourth grades."

While incidents such as these are unfortunate, they do serve to remind us that parents *want* and *need* to be informed about their child's education. Furthermore, they have a right not only to be informed about educational practices but also to question practices that have not been adequately explained. It is our job as educators to explain our beliefs and practices so that most parents and community members will feel both informed and comfortable with the methods and materials used to educate tomorrow's citizens. As responsible educators, we have to keep abreast of the needs of children who will work and live in the twenty-first century and of research concerning the best, most effective teaching and learning practices. So too must we accept responsibility for transmitting this critical information to parents and other members of the community.

A NOTE FROM ELIZABETH . . .

In any setting, when changes occur there are always those who feel threatened or uncertain as to how the changes will affect them. We cannot assume that teachers and parents will simply "go along" without questioning the changes that are being advocated. Teachers may think that the changes to be implemented are, in actuality, a criticism of their past practices. Or they may fear that the changes will result in more of a time commitment than they are willing to make. Parents, because they are familiar with traditional instructional practices, may feel uncomfortable with new practices they perceive as "experimental."

For administrators to try to slip through changes without securing the understanding and support of the individuals involved would be both unwise and counterproductive. Accomplishing this task involves the development of a plan of action for clearly facing the issues that will arise. As the "front line" person, the administrator must possess a solid knowledge base and be able to convey a clear rationale for changes that are to take place. While classroom teachers are in the best position for disseminating information about the specific strategies employed in their classrooms, the administrator must be able to "speak the same language" when confronted by parents and members of the public.

Despite some evidence to the contrary, the American public wants to see the development of a strong educational system. According to the most recent Gallup poll of the public's attitudes toward the public schools (Eman, Rose, & Gallup, 1991): Only weeks after a military victory in the Persian Gulf, less than half (41 percent) of poll respondents considered "building the strongest military force in the world" to be very important. By contrast, 89 percent regarded "developing the most efficient education system in the world" as very important. Further, the respondents favored (by 62 percent to 33 percent) parental and student choice in public schools and paying more for teaching that is deemed to be particularly effective (69 percent to 24 percent). With respect to curriculum and testing, a wide majority (81 percent) favored the adoption of national achievement standards and goals and the use of standardized national tests (77 percent).

There has been a great deal of talk and debate over the last few years concerning the six national goals for education that were first announced in February 1990 by the Bush administration and the strategy for achieving these goals by the year 2000. The Bush plan calls for a number of elements for school improvement, including a "voluntary" national system of achievement testing; parental choice of the school their children will attend; merit pay for teaching "core" subjects such as English, math, science, history, and geography; and the creation of what have been termed "New American Schools" and "America 2000 communities." The Clinton campaign literature indicated that his administration would strongly support a pro-child agenda. Such an agenda appears most likely to have a significant effect on the health and development of children at the pre-K level.

In previous chapters we discussed the empowerment of principals, teachers, and students. Ernest Boyer (1991), in his book *Ready to Learn: A Mandate for the Nation,* states, "For all children to come to school ready to learn, we must empower parents" (p. 46). He encourages organized preschool parent-teacher organizations and a parent education program that reflects the best practices. With respect to communities, Boyer advocates "neighborhoods for learning." He states, "To give children the space they need for growth and exploration, we recommend that a network of well-designed outdoor and indoor parks be created in every community" (p. 91) and that "shopping malls include in their facilities a Ready-to-Learn Center where young children can engage in play and learning" (p. 91). He also recommends that schools, through after-school and preschool programs, be used as "Ready-to-Learn Centers" open to people of all ages who work with young children. While Boyer focuses specifically on the role of parents and community during a child's early years, this involvement should not decrease as the child grows. Rather, families are encouraged to be active participants in the entire educational process [EQUALS, 1986; Northwest EQUALS, 1988; Cochran, M., & Henderson, C. R. (1987)].

Clearly, since the public is interested in our schools' policies and procedures, there is a critical need to educate all players in both the public and political realms. In chapter three we discussed the change process and the activities that promote positive change, such as effective staff development activities and district- and schoolwide planning. In this chapter we will discuss current research in the area of parent and community involvement and the need to assess the assets and liabilities each school brings to a three-way partnership between the home, school, and community. We will also describe strategies for building and maintaining solid parental and public communication and for garnering the support needed to bring about positive changes. In addition, we will address parent education, suggesting possible topics as well as various means of presenting them.

What Research Tells Us about the Importance of Forging Strong Home-School-Community Relationships

Ample documentation exists concerning the effectiveness of parent involvement in improving school competency and students' attitudes from early childhood through adolescence (Epstein, 1986; Powell, 1986; Dembo, Sweitzer, & Lauritzen, 1985; Henderson, 1987). Although few parents participate at the school building level or in school decision-making activities (Bauch, 1988; Dornbusch & Ritter, 1988), most parents do report occasionally helping their children at home, even though they are not always certain whether they are "doing things right" (Epstein, 1990).

According to research conducted by Epstein (1986) and Dauber and Epstein (1989), over 90 percent of parents of elementary and middle-grade pupils believe that teachers should tell parents how to help their children at home; and many low-income and less-educated parents report a need to know more about the school program in order to help their children. As stated by Epstein (1990), "All or most parents in all types of schools and at all grade levels express the need for clear communications about their children's attendance, behavior, academic progress, the content of what their children are learning, and how to help their children at home" (p. 109). Further, teachers who actively seek parents' involvement are considered to be more effective teachers. Those parents, when surveyed by Epstein (1985, 1986), were significantly more likely than other parents to say that they: (1) believed parents should help their children at home; (2) understood more about what their child was learning in school than they had in past years; and (3) received many ideas about how to help their children at home. In addition, these parents rated their child's teacher higher in overall teaching ability and interpersonal skills than did parents of children whose teachers did not actively seek parental support and involvement.

As stated by Moles (1987), "Parent involvement in education is an idea whose time has come" (p. 137). Not only does research evidence reveal the contributions that well-designed programs of parent involvement make toward student achievement, it also yields important and useful information for schools and districts that are developing comprehensive parent and community involvement programs.

In their book *Beyond the Bake Sale: An Educator's Guide to Working with Parents*, authors Henderson, Marburger, and Ooms (1986) list five roles that parents play in the education of their children. The first role is that of *partner,* in which the parents perform "basic obligations for their child's education and social development" (p. 3). When serving in the role of *collaborator* or *problem solver,* the parents "stimulate and reinforce learning by providing a variety of enrichment activities" (p. 3) such as reading aloud to their child, taking the child to museums and libraries, and so forth. This role involves the parent in activities that are traditionally most closely associated with the role of the classroom teacher. Though referred to by the authors as roles that parents perform, the other three roles could be assumed by both parents and members of the community at large. These roles are: (1) *audience,* which involves "attending and appreciating the school's performance and productions"; (2) *supporters*—those who provide "volunteer assistance to teachers, the parent organization, and to other parents"; and (3) *advisors and/or co-decision makers*—those who provide "input on school policy and program through membership in ad hoc or permanent governance bodies" (p. 3).

Members of the community as well as parents have both a right and a responsibility to become actively involved in the education of tomorrow's citizens. According to the twenty-third annual Gallup poll (Elam, et al., 1991), in response to the question "How much interest do you have in what is going on in the local public schools?" 76 percent of the respondents reported either "quite a lot" or "some." Only 24 percent of the respondents answered "very little" or "none at all." Yet when asked about their participation in school-related activities and events, 49 percent of the sample population reported that they had not been involved at all during the past year. This was in spite of 69 percent of the respondents feeling that they knew "quite a lot" or "some" about their local public schools. As stated in the report, "More significant for educators, however, is the fact that the more people know about their schools, the more likely they are to support and defend them. Correspondingly, the more interest people have in the schools and the more they participate in school-related activities, the more likely they are to support and defend the schools" (p. 53).

As schools and systems face declining funds and increasingly tight budgets, we must not underestimate the "power of the people" in determining how monies for public education are allocated. In most communities the majority of voters do not have children in school. Of the 1,500 adults who responded to the Gallup poll, 68 percent had no children in school, yet 64 percent favored awarding more state and federal funds to schools that showed progress, within a reasonable time, toward the national goals. Further, 57 percent favored not renewing the contracts of principals and teachers in schools that do not show progress within a reasonable amount of time.

Barriers to Creating and Maintaining Strong Partnerships

Many schools accidentally construct barriers that prevent parents from becoming actively involved. Common examples include the scheduling of parent-teacher conferences and special assemblies and programs only during the school day (when most parents are working), lack of child care during conferences and other school events, and failure to send newsletters and other communications to noncustodial parents. Another major barrier is the lack of time, particularly in single-parent households and households where both parents work full-time.

Since research findings consistently support increased involvement of parents in their children's education, it would appear that all classrooms and all schools would welcome a strong partnership with both parents and community members and that all school personnel would work diligently to overcome barriers to parent and community involvement. Unfortunately, this is not the case (Henderson, et al., 1986). One of the major barriers to involvement is teachers' and administrators' lack of interest. In one school, every fall the principal stands before the parents during the first open house and tells them that because of the way the school is run, there is no need for a parent-teacher organization. Schools such as this one can be easily spotted by the sign that is usually located near the front entrance to the building. The sign typically reads "STOP! ALL VISITORS ARE TO REPORT TO THE OFFICE." Attitude barriers such as these perpetuate the battle for "turf" between parents and teachers and stand in the way of the changes that need to be made before strong partnerships can be forged. While we will not dwell on this issue, we do urge each school administrator to take steps to identify and eradicate barriers to parent and community involvement.

Determining Your School's "PCQ" or "Parent-Community Quotient"

The Random House Dictionary defines *quotient* as "the result obtained by dividing one number into another." In terms of effective home-school-community relationships, we might think of a school's PCQ as the level of parent and community involvement in that school, which, when calculated into the total experiences that contribute to each child's education, results in an improvement in student attitudes, student successes, and rates of retention. A high PCQ should also give the school a positive image and the support and trust of the parents and community.

What factors help determine PCQ? To answer this question we will look at the characteristics of schools that have already established strong relationships with parents and members of the community (Henderson, et al., 1986; Chrispeels, 1991; Dulaney, 1987; Berger, 1981). These shared characteristics involve (1) the establishment of effective communication with all parents; (2) a variety of parent education offerings aimed at helping parents more effectively participate in their children's education; (3) a strong connection to community resources as well as strategies for forging positive community relations; (4) support for and coordination of activities enabling school staff and parents to implement and sustain long-term involvement; and (5) ways to include parents in decision-making activities.

A beneficial activity for members of the school staff might be to brainstorm a list of all of the ways that the needs discussed above are currently being addressed. They might then write a list of ways to expand on these areas. Similarly, the staff might brainstorm a list of possible barriers to more effective parent and community involvement and then construct a list of possible ways to overcome or compensate for each barrier. For example, a school newsletter, while helpful in providing information to parents, is generally a one-way communication. The staff may decide to include a "What's on Your Mind?" section and to encourage parents to respond with comments, questions, or suggestions. Additionally, school newsletters are generally sent only to parents of children enrolled in the school. As a useful public relations tool, the school newsletter could be delivered to area businesses, real estate offices, and so forth. School newsletters also make good reading material for waiting rooms of doctors' and dentists' offices. The lists that are generated through these brainstorming sessions would be used to plan a more comprehensive parent and community involvement program. Another activity might involve categorizing existing activities according to the various role groups specified by Henderson, et al. (1986). Those roles that lack activities are a natural place to begin work. According to Henderson, et al. (1986), in schools "where the principal and faculty have a strong commitment to working in partnership with parents, all these types of parent involvement flourish and reinforce each other" (p. 13). Additionally, school administrators and teachers are advised to determine their priorities for parent involvement based on a number of issues, including whether the most pressing concern is an immediate "payoff" in student achievement or a need to "boost the image of" the school in the community, stretch limited resources further, or build a stronger school program.

In an effort to get a more accurate and personalized reading of the public's opinion of their school, some schools conduct their own surveys. These surveys may take the form of telephone surveys such as the one in figure 5.1.

Some schools prefer to use "report cards" on which the parents and/or community members grade various components of the school program. These report cards can be mailed or even published in the local newspaper and can be designed in a number of ways to obtain various kinds of information. For example, the one shown in figure 5.2 includes a place for individuals to volunteer to perform various services for the school.

Surveys such as those in figures 5.1 and 5.2 can yield important information about how a school is viewed by the community. They also let the public know that we need and value their opinions and their contributions. We cannot afford to wait until a couple of months before an election to start a public relations campaign. We must begin immediately to establish a comprehensive program for involving nonparental members of our communities in our schools. The "public" includes, but is certainly not limited to: senior citizens, grandparents, high school and college students, businesses,

Figure 5.1

PARENT/COMMUNITY SURVEY

By Phone: Hello, this is _____. I'm a volunteer calling for the _____ school. We're conducting a telephone survey to find out what parent and other community members think about our school. May I have five to ten minutes of your time to ask you a few important questions?

1. To begin, how many years have you lived in this school district?
   - a) less than one year
   - b) 1-3 years
   - c) 4-6 years
   - d) 7-10 years
   - e) 11 or more years

2. Have you had any children graduate from our school?
   - a) yes
   - b) no

3. Do you currently have school-aged children?
   - a) yes
   - b) no

4. If yes, what grades are they in? _____

5. Students are often awarded grades of A, B, C, D, F. If you were to grade our school in the same way, what grade would you award?
   - a) A
   - b) B
   - c) C
   - d) D
   - e) F

6. Where do you get most of your information about our school?
   - a) my children
   - b) students
   - c) newspapers
   - d) other adults/friends/relatives
   - e) radio
   - f) television
   - g) school newsletter/publications
   - h) other (please specify)

7. In the past year, have you: (Check all that apply.)
   - a) attended a school event
   - b) been asked to volunteer services for the school
   - c) served as a school volunteer
   - d) participated in a Parent-Teacher Association meeting
   - e) supported the school through fund-raising activities
   - f) attended a school open house
   - g) visited with your child's teacher

8. Overall, to what degree do you feel you know about the school's present curriculum and instructional programs?
   - a) I have a very high degree of information
   - b) I have a high degree of information
   - c) I have a fair degree of information
   - d) I have a low degree of information

9. How important do you feel it is for you to receive information about the
   school's curriculum and instructional program?
   a) very important
   b) important
   c) somewhat important
   d) not very important

Now I'm going to read a list of programs and services offered by our school. As I read each item, tell me if you think that our school should give more attention, less attention, or about the same amount of attention to each one.

10. Reading. Should our school give more, less or about the same emphasis to reading?	MORE	LESS	SAME
11. Writing.	MORE	LESS	SAME
12. Computer literacy.	MORE	LESS	SAME
13. Mathematical reasoning.	MORE	LESS	SAME
14. Parent education	MORE	LESS	SAME
15. Public relations	MORE	LESS	SAME
16. Home-school communication	MORE	LESS	SAME
17. Corrective/remedial reading and math programs	MORE	LESS	SAME
18. Gifted education	MORE	LESS	SAME
19. Counseling	MORE	LESS	SAME

In this last section, I'm going to read you a list of statements. After I read each one, please tell me if you tend to agree, disagree, or feel neutral about each one.

20. Most students like attending _____ school.	AGREE	DISAGREE	NEUTRAL
21. The teachers in _____ school use up-to-date methods and materials.	AGREE	DISAGREE	NEUTRAL
22. The principal motivates and supports the teachers.	AGREE	DISAGREE	NEUTRAL
23. Students who have difficulty learning can get extra help in our school.	AGREE	DISAGREE	NEUTRAL
24. Students with special talents and abilities are motivated through appropriately challenging and enriching learning activities.	AGREE	DISAGREE	NEUTRAL
25. The school climate is friendly and inviting.	AGREE	DISAGREE	NEUTRAL
26. Overall, I am pleased with what I know about _____ school.	AGREE	DISAGREE	NEUTRAL

Figure 5.2

REPORT CARD FOR _____ SCHOOL

DIRECTIONS: Please rate our school's performance in each area.

	EXCELLENT	GOOD	AVERAGE	POOR	UNDECIDED
CURRICULUM & INSTRUCTION					
* Teacher effectiveness					
* Up-to-date instructional methods used					
* Up-to-date materials used					
* Program effectiveness in meeting individual needs					
SCHOOL CLIMATE & PHYSICAL FACILITIES					
* Open, inviting atmosphere					
* Orderly and appropriate student conduct					
* Attractive, well-kept grounds					
* Attractive, well-kept building					
PARENT-COMMUNITY INVOLVEMENT					
* Home-School Communications					
* Parent-Teacher Conferences					
* Parent Education					
* Public Relations					
SPECIAL PROGRAMS					
* Corrective/Remedial Reading/ Math					
* Speech & Language					
* Gifted					
ADMINISTRATION					
* Available					
* Open, caring attitude					
* Knowledgeable					
* Effectiveness					

merchants, teachers, retired teachers, youth groups, legislators, military personnel, service and civic organizations, and new residents. We must tap the resources of the individuals that make up these various groups and garner their support for our schools. We can do this by sending them our school newsletters, by keeping current displays on bulletin boards in shopping malls and grocery stores, and by submitting weekly newspaper and radio news briefs, to name just a few of the many ways to keep the public informed. Some

PARENT-COMMUNITY INVOLVEMENT

_____ school is YOUR school! Please check any of the following areas in which you would be willing to offer services.

_____Listen to students read

_____Read to children

_____Tutor (under teacher's supervision)

_____Make classroom aids

_____Type/word process

_____Bind books

_____Share a talent or career experience

_____Provide transporation on field trips

_____Provide child care services during school events (at school building)

_____Provide transportation to parents for conferences

_____Provide photocopying services

_____Other: (Please specify)

schools have special days set aside for different groups to tour the school: senior citizens' day, grandparents' day, local merchants' day, bankers' day, retired teachers' day, and so forth. The usual agenda for these special days involves a coffee-and-donut hour followed by a tour of the school (perhaps conducted by student volunteers) and a discussion of the school curriculum and programs. The participants might also receive follow-up information about the school and the various volunteer services that the school needs.

Schools and school systems that have taken the time to organize these personal contacts find that they are very helpful in garnering public support. Again, these should not be just "one-shot" activities but rather a series of ongoing events aimed at helping the public understand both the strengths and needs of _their_ schools. To this end, school personnel must commit themselves to maintaining a healthy relationship with all players – students, parents, and members of the community.

Because the Oakwood staff realize the value of an informed public, they seek creative ways to link the community with their classrooms. For example, the first-grade classes involve community leaders in serving as "reading role models" for the children. The mayor, chief of police, dentists, doctors, business people, local football heroes, and others are asked to visit the classrooms to read to the children and talk about how they use reading in their private and professional lives. A local dentist read *Dr. DeSoto,* William Steig's enchanting tale of a mouse-dentist who outwits a fox, and then talked about reading's importance to a dentist.

Besides having community members come into the school, the children often go out into the community to share their reading, writing, and projects. By accepting invitations to present programs to the Lions, Rotary, or women's clubs, the students enjoy the spotlight and have a wonderful opportunity to spread information about the school.

The children also reach out to the community through many and varied letter-writing activities throughout the year. Children write to pen pals in area nursing homes and to local politicians for information or to express opinions on local issues. Oakwood's theme of "Caretakers of the Earth" inspired many letters on environmental topics, including letters to the editor of the local newspaper. All these letter-writing activities create a bond between the school community and the outside community.

Communicating with Parents and Community Members

Just as it is the right and responsibility of each citizen to become involved in public education, so is it the responsibility of professionals in the field of education to inform these citizens about the strengths and liabilities of today's schools. Making the move toward implementing a whole language program is a strength, and members of the community need to understand and support this move. With our strengths come some liabilities, one of which is the lack of trade books, educational resources, and other materials that support and enhance whole language learning. Another liability for most systems is the lack of media specialists and librarians to help classroom teachers plan and implement various units of study.

Schools and school districts need to give the public the information it needs to make informed judgments about the educational system. In a successful attempt to enlighten both parents and community members, the Board of Education of Hannibal Public Schools, Missouri, sponsored an open forum called "Questions and Answers about Whole Language." The entire community was invited. The evening began with a general statement by the superintendent of schools about the history of whole language in the district and how it was evolving from the point of view of the central office. This address was followed by a series of informational sessions (see figure 5.3) conducted by classroom teachers. Participants attended two half-hour

Figure 5.3

OPEN FORUM -
QUESTIONS AND ANSWERS ABOUT WHOLE LANGUAGE
HANNIBAL PUBLIC SCHOOLS
JANUARY 9, 1990

Agenda

7:00 - Welcome by Superintendent Dr. Scott Taveau

7:15 - Small Group Informational Sessions (Choose 2)

LITERATURE-BASED READING INSTRUCTION - Room 218
Linda Huss and Julie Hart
Literature is an integral part of a whole language reading program. The teaching of reading through literature will be explained.

WRITING PROCESS - Large Group Instruction Room
Penny Strube, Beth Taylor, and Jana Suchland
The application of skills is an important part of a whole language program. How skills such as word usage, sentence structure, grammar, etc., are taught and reinforced in a writing program will be discussed.

INTEGRATED CURRICULUM - Room 219
Suzanne Gottman and Carol Davis
Reading and writing across the content areas are emphasized in whole language classrooms. The integration of reading and writing in the subjects of science and social studies will be explained.

ISSUES IN WHOLE LANGUAGE - Room 211
Jill Janes and Mary Skinner
This session will deal with misconceptions about whole language teaching. The primary focus will be spelling and phonics instruction.

7:45 - Small group informational session
Repeat of above sessions

8:15 - Panel Discussion - Large Group Instruction Room
Scott Taveau, Larry Roberts, Ron Mack, Jill Janes, Penny Strube, Julie Hart, and Linda Huss

---

sessions during which teachers explained the changes that were taking place in their classrooms. These sessions were followed by a panel discussion in the school auditorium. Since participants had already had an opportunity to speak directly with teachers about such issues as phonics, spelling, writing, and grammar, the general atmosphere was extremely positive. In fact, the most common reaction was "Is that what whole language is? It makes sense to me."

A NOTE FROM ELIZABETH . . .

As the school principal, it is critical that you know and understand the theory behind the instruction that is taking place. Parents consider you responsible for what is happening in the classroom and it is up to you to know and to be able to communicate the information they need. In a whole language school parents will probably question why there is so little use of traditional textbooks, or why there are so few workbook and skill pages going home. While the teachers will, in many circumstances, want to meet with the parents to discuss issues in more detail, it is critical that the administrator be able and willing to discuss issues in a knowledgeable manner. Parents lose confidence in a principal whose standard reply is "You'll have to ask your child's teacher."

When the lines of communication are open, we can avoid many of the pitfalls and misunderstandings that occur when new practices are implemented. One kindergarten teacher used to complain about "ditto moms," mothers who, when their oldest child was in kindergarten, received a daily or weekly stack of "dittoes." These dittoes were considered evidence of a strong academic kindergarten. In a whole language classroom, dittoes are seldom if ever used. Parents who have come to expect this type of feedback from the teacher need to be helped to understand how and why the program has changed. They also need to receive other types of feedback about their child's education. At Oakwood parents are often "audiences." Serving in this role gives parents an important opportunity to observe what their children are learning and increases the children's experience increased motivation to do good work. For example, the products of theme studies are always videotaped. The children can take the tapes home for their parents to see. The tapes may show the children reading reports or newspapers, acting in plays, or explaining timelines or other products they have created. By viewing the videos, the parents receive important information about their child's development as a researcher, reader, writer, and speaker. The parents can also gain information about areas that need improvement.

Teachers also send out newsletters. Although the newsletters vary from classroom to classroom, articles written by the children are quite typical. Figure 5.4 shows the September issue of *Good News Bears*, the first-grade newsletter. The children engaged in purposeful, meaningful writing as they created pieces that conveyed particular information to the audience—their parents.

Parents also serve as audiences for classroom sharing times, which are scheduled after the monthly P.T.A. meetings. The entire family is invited to actively participate in these meetings. For example, the teacher and children in each classroom might plan a literature study night. On one such night at Oakwood, the families convened in the classrooms after the P.T.A. meeting. Some rooms had requested that parents read an assignment before the literature study night; others had asked the parents and children to produce a

Figure 5.4

GOOD NEWS BEARS

SEPTEMBER ISSUE

First Grade Newsletter   Oakwood School   Hannibal, Missouri

Book Review by Vick

BUSY STREET

Busy Street is a funny book. I like the book because it is a number book. It's about kids and workers. I love all the books in my class - even the new books.

SPIDERS
by Jamie Bush

I know they spin webs. I know they eat other bugs. They are not insects, because insects hae six legs and spiders have eight legs.

First Grade
by Cammie Greathouse

We do numbers. Today we are doing o's. Reading is fun. We do literature books, but the fun thing is journals. We have Art. We are finishing our lambs.

MATH
by Kim Menze

We have been learning about patterns and counting pennies. We have been learning other things.

ASHLEY'S SNAKE

I found a garter snake. I put it in a bucket to take to school. We read about snakes. Garter snakes don't harm people. They live in back yards and parks. Baby garter snakes like earthworms, but when they grow up they eat frogs and fish.

By Ashley McClain

Bears by Carrie Perrin

Bears like berries. Brown bears like honey. Polar bears like seals. Bears like insects. Their mom takes their babies away from danger.

OUR CLASS
by Kristina Shrode

In Mrs. Ingebretson's room we write our names on our eating chart. We do math tubbing with unifix cubes and play dough. We build with blocks. We make patterns with shapes. We go to the library and music. We go to art and P. E. I like to go to lunch best.

TEACHER FEATURE

A NOTE FROM MRS. ZAHNER

You may have heard your child discuss "tubbing" for math. This year the children are learning through discovery. We teach counting, patterns, sorting, and classifying, comparing, graphing, etc. through working with manipulatives. They see and experince. We won't be sending home a lot of worksheets.

For reading the children choose a book that interests them and we do projects related to their story. We have been reading about bears and Mother Goose nursery rhymes.

If you would like to volunteer to listen to children read, help type stories, etc., give your child's teacher a call.

MUSIC CLASS
by Josh Britt

In Music class with Mrs. Mead we sing funny songs. We also sing l-o-o-n-g songs.

MATH CLASS
by Elizabeth Gentry

We have tubs. We do our fat math books. We do skinny math books too. Most of all I like lunch.

WRITING STORIES
By Audrey Pickett

We write stories every day. We read stories to a friend and edit our stories.. Then we get our book published. I type my stories and journal on the typewriter.

NEWS FROM AROUND FIRST GRADE CLASSES

We have tubbing stations. One of the centers is unifix cubes. They are little blocks that you hook together. We have pattern blocks and play dough.

By Shawna Epperson

WHAT WE DO

We make shapes in P. E. We make pictures. We say the pledge. We eat lunch. We go out.

By Sarah Ellis

MOTHER GOOSE

We have been learning about Mother Goose and we like it. We make and color pictures about those people like Old King Cole and Little Miss Muffett.

by Kelly Milam

UPCOMING EVENTS

October 9 - Sales brochures due.

October 17 - P. T. A. After meeting, parents and students go to classroom for presentations and programs.

project to share with the group. During the evening the parents gained first-hand knowledge of what literature study is all about as well as training on how to listen to children read. The music teacher demonstrated what she was teaching the children, and the children demonstrated what they had learned. Then parents and siblings were taught the same songs. The art teacher talked about skill development and asked parents to look at the children's art, which the children explained. The P.E. teacher asked children to demonstrate their P.E. curriculum. Parents participated with their children in dancing, gymnastics, jumping rope, and so on. In the spring the school holds an exposition of the children's work in science and social studies. Tables and booths set up around the gym enable parents to view the projects the children created throughout the year while studying the schoolwide theme. For example, the "Caretakers of the Earth" theme resulted in books, posters, fund-raising activities, recycling projects, and videos.

Realizing that face-to-face communication is the most important tool for parent and community involvement, the faculty and students at Oakwood also host several special days throughout the year. The Mothers' and Grandmothers' Day Tea is planned around Mothers' Day to inspire children to write poetry, songs, and stories about mothers and grandmothers. Children also interview grandparents, which results in wonderful biographies that they share on this day. The children also experience what it means to host a party by planning and serving the refreshments. This special day gives parents a valuable view of the community to which their child belongs.

Father Goose Day, held over a lunch hour, is a day for fathers and grandfathers to eat with the children. After lunch the children take their visitors to the classroom to participate in an activity or project, or the teacher may ask a father to read a story to the class.

On Notable Day the children come to school dressed as the person in a biography they have written. Parents are invited to visit the classroom to hear the children read the biographies, or they may take home the videotape the children have produced.

To develop a truly effective system of communication it is important that the entire school staff contribute to a planned effort. Some schools and teachers find it helpful to keep a special calendar just for recording home-school communications. As busy school personnel, we find it all too easy to forget to keep in touch with each child's parent. Jotting down each communication is often all we need to jog our memories. For example, when we call Susan's mother to discuss an upcoming field trip, we make a note on our calendar. Similarly, if newsletters or want ads for classroom supplies are sent home, this information is recorded. Teachers will want to take stock every now and then to assess whether they are communicating with each family and whether they are making ample provisions for two-way communication.

As suggested in the preceding section, some one-way communication tools can easily be revised to ensure opportunities for two-way communication. Additionally, parent-teacher conferences, telephone conversations, and open houses also provide time for effective two-way communication.

Parent Education

One of the major goals of a whole language school is to convince parents that they can help their children learn to use language by involving the children in the same sorts of routine tasks that they themselves do. It takes a total school effort to make parents understand that what they have to offer their children is important and valuable and that it is very similar to what a whole language classroom offers. Teaching parents the strategies that are used in a whole language classroom is not difficult once the parents understand that we teach children in ways that can be immediately applied in everyday life. We do not ask children to memorize lists of words from a spelling text; rather, we ask them to identify misspelled words in their writing and to study those words so that they can spell them correctly in their future writing. We do not ask them to read aloud to us so that we can determine whether or not they can pronounce all of the words correctly; instead, we ask them to practice reading orally so that they can inform or entertain their listeners.

We must also convey, however, what we mean when we speak of developmental appropriateness so that parents understand the importance of a curriculum that is developmentally appropriate for each child. For example, teachers of young children must spend time discussing with parents the developmental nature of spelling. When parents understand the stages of writing development, from prephonetic to phonetic or approximated spelling to transitional and conventional spelling, they can reinforce and encourage their young writer. Thus children's growth is fostered both at home and at school.

A NOTE FROM ELIZABETH . . .

Probably the most difficult thing we have had to overcome is the idea that pain must be associated with learning. Because the children at Oakwood love school, parents wonder if it is hard enough for them. We work to share with parents the growth that their children are making. When they see that the products created by children in whole language classrooms far exceed those produced in a traditional program, they come to realize that if children are motivated with a purpose that fits their individual needs, learning is both fun and productive! People often ask,

One of the many ways that Oakwood teachers encourage parents to practice reading with their children involves a "Reading Report Card" that is sent home with first-grade pupils every week (see figure 5.5). The report card has two parts. The first part is divided into days of the week, and parents place a star under the day(s) they read to their child. The second part has a place for both parent and student to sign verifying that the child read the literature book; then the parent assesses the child's reading performance.

Classroom teachers are in the best position to share with parents specific ways to promote learning in the home. Oakwood teachers put together a loose-leaf notebook that parents can take home. The notebooks contain a continually updated collection of articles on child development and other subjects. They also contain examples of checklists that the teachers use to assess children's progress as well as explanations of these instruments. In addition, the notebook has explanatory statements about many whole language issues, such as skills instruction, phonics, spelling, and comprehension. Many teachers have found that their parent education notebook is so popular that they have made several copies of it.

Most teachers also send home letters explaining various aspects of their program. These letters (see figure 5.6) enlighten the parent about the specifics of the program and provide a means for suggesting related activities to do at home.

A more traditional means of parent education, the parent workshop, has been increasingly emphasized during the past few years, especially since so many schools and districts have begun prekindergarten programs. Funding for these and many other programs at "innovative schools" usually requires plans for parent involvement in general and for parent education in particular.

As Joyce Epstein (1988) states, "Schools . . . have begun to move from *telling* parents that their involvement is important to *showing* them that their involvement is permitted and encouraged and then *guiding* them in specific ways to assist in their child's development and learning" (p. 58). Through a strong parent education component we can show parents strategies for working with their children, and we can guide them in applying these strategies appropriately. As a required project for a university course in parent and community involvement, groups of undergraduate and graduate students present one-hour parent education workshops on a Saturday morning late in the semester. This "Saturday School" for parents has been very popular for a number of reasons. From among a variety of workshops on interesting and practical topics, parents choose two. Each workshop involves a small amount of

Figure 5.5

READING REPORT CARD

Parents of (student's name) _____

Date

First Grade, Oakwood Elementary School, Mrs. Davis, Room 106

Dear Parents,

In order to provide a better reading/learning environment for your child, I am asking that you read to him/her a MINIMUM of 15 minutes daily. In order to keep track of your reading schedule, I will be sending each week in the weekly packet this report card for you to fill out each day and return the next week. Please place a star under the day(s) you read to your child.

Sun.   Mon.   Tues.   Wed .   Thurs.   Fri.   Sat.

Parent Signature_____

Student Signature_____

Please listen to your child "read" the literature book he/she brings home each week and then decide which sentence BEST describes his/her reading.

     1. My child was hesitant to read and needed help.
     2. My child needed some help on about 1/2 the words.
     3. My child could read about 90% of the book without my help.
     4. My child read the book with GREAT enthusiasm and knew all
        the words.

NUMBER _____

***** Return with weekly packet on Monday.*****

theory, or "why this is a good idea," followed by hands-on activities. In one of the most popular arrangements, the participants gather in groups to take part in a variety of "learning center" activities. Each activity lasts for approximately ten minutes, after which the groups move on to other centers. At the centers, parents get firsthand experience with strategies that they can use with their children. Frequently, the centers have inexpensive materials from which parents can make simple games and learning activities to take home.

     Another reason for the success of these workshops is the interaction between the workshop leaders and the participants and also among the participants themselves. To accomplish this, name tags are provided, ice breakers are used to help relax and unify the participants, child care and

Figure 5.6

LETTER TO PARENTS
*Progress is developmental
and practice makes the significant difference.*

Dear Parents,

In first grade, I try to create an atmosphere that encourages writing. The children will be engaged in purposeful writing throughout the day.

Early in the day, the children write in their personal journals, addressing their comments or stories to me. Often children will fill two to three seventy-page notebooks during the year. I use the entries to follow the progress that the children are making as well as keeping up with what is important to them. The journals will all be returned to you at the end of the year and will be a record of your child's growth that I know you'll cherish.

Also during the time that I am meeting with smaller groups for reading, the children will be engaged in a number of writing activities: note writing, making birthday, get well or thank you cards, making posters, advertisements, poems and other projects assigned that go along with their literature book for the week (Lit Projects).

There will also be a time for book publishing, where the children will be shown and led through the entire writing process.

Later in the year, as children study a variety of science, social studies and health concepts, they will get experience in note taking and report writing.

The range of children's writing varies tremendously, but I accept and encourage each child at his or her developmental level. Most children begin with sound/symbol knowledge of most of the consonants and will write the first letter of each word. Some will write random streams of letters without spacing; some write with spelling very close to conventional spelling. Regardless of where your child is developmentally she or he will be given the opportunity to grow as a writer.

In this type of environment, writing improves through daily use, practice and guidance. Handwriting and fine motor skills develop rapidly through daily writing. The formation of letters is formally taught, but not overemphasized during self-selected writing. Conventions of print, spelling and language patterns develop through repeated practice. Confidence and skills grow as student writing is shared.

Encourage your child to practice writing and celebrate the progress.

Sincerely,

Mrs. Paula Ingebretson

Mrs. Paula Ingebretson

---

refreshments are available, and parents move around freely during at least a portion of each workshop. Additionally, the participants receive attractively prepared written materials about the entire workshop, lessening the burden of writing down or remembering what was said and done.

At Oakwood, parents participating in discussion groups learn how to help their children as they read with them. Although these discussion groups are sometimes held during the day, they are most often scheduled at night, when most parents are free to attend. During the discussions teachers talk to parents about reading for meaning and about the stages through which children progress as they develop into mature, capable readers. Often this helps parents realize that some behaviors, such as a young child pretending to read by reciting a story from memory, are normal stages in reading development. These discussions are also a good way to introduce parents to good literature. In fact, parents of older children find that they benefit a great deal from the ideas suggested as topics for literature discussion with their children. Teachers have even been told that the literature discussions in the home have helped some parent-child relationships.

Workshop and discussion topics would, of course, vary from school to school and from district to district. Included in the list of offerings could be topics related to the school or district agenda, such as "Understanding and Supporting Our Kindergarten Writing Program" or "Literature Study Groups: What You Can Do to Help." Of course, also included would be topics parents have expressed an interest in. Typically, these include such topics as positive discipline, inexpensive family field trips, and nutritious, tasty, easy-to-make meals on a budget. At Oakwood, programs that highlight the newest and best in children's literature are always well attended. Often teachers offer their services to study groups in the community, sharing advice about good literature for children of various ages. In addition, book fairs, held twice yearly at Oakwood, educate parents about the importance of reading at home. Parents can browse and shop for books and talk to the teachers who are on hand to offer suggestions and advice.

Ideally, the topics included in the parent education programs should come from a combination of school or district needs, such as the need to tell parents about the new strategies or materials that comprise the school's literacy program, as well as from parent needs. Parent needs can be determined through written surveys, telephone interviews, suggestion boxes placed in the schools, "graffiti" parent bulletin boards where parents can write messages and notes to each other, and meetings and group discussions.

Methods of delivering parent education can be as extensive as the topics themselves. Traditional media such as newspapers, radio, and television can be combined with more creative, nontraditional methods such as placing brochures and pamphlets in waiting rooms of doctors' and dentists' offices, mailing brochures and pamphlets with bank statements or bills from local merchants, providing a parent education area in the local library, and printing various parent education "tips" on the sides of milk and soft drink cartons, and so on, when there are local distributors of these products.

Parent education is essential to the success of any effort at parent-community involvement in the schools. As we have demonstrated, there are many vehicles for delivering information and sharing strategies. While all of the options we describe require resources (primarily time and energy), they are effective. With effective parent education come trust and support. And with trust and support come many benefits for children and school personnel alike.

School Volunteers

Although not easy to do, finding people who are willing to volunteer their services during the school day is another way to communicate with parents and other school volunteers. Service organizations, senior citizens' groups, retired teachers, parents, grandparents, and others have donated countless hours of service to schools. Even volunteers who can give only a few hours a week become better informed about the school and its curriculum.

Volunteers serve in a variety of ways, including being mentors at learning centers, helping publish books, reading and talking to children, and listening to children read. When working at learning centers, volunteers serve as organizers, encouragers, and facilitators. Through their involvement they gain a rich understanding of the learning that takes place as children work to construct their own meaning. Volunteers who help children publish books may do this in the school or at home. Publishing books generally involves typing the edited pieces and putting them between cardboard covers. These volunteers are often surprised at both the quantity and quality of children's writing at all grade levels.

When parents volunteer to listen to children read at school, the teacher suggests some responses to the children that will make the time more enjoyable and productive. The volunteer also learns important information about the stages in reading development. Children look forward to the volunteers coming to listen to them read. Oftentimes fathers who work the night shift will take time to come during the day. This is a special treat for many children!

Another part of the volunteer program at Oakwood is called V.I.P., which stands for Very Important Parent. This is a variation of Career Day, which is sponsored by the third-grade classes. Each child signs up a parent or relative to be the V.I.P. for a certain time. On the designated day the parent or relative comes to school to explain and if possible demonstrate her or his job. On V.I.P. days the third-grade classes have arranged flowers, toured a fire truck and an ambulance, spread a spinnaker on the lawn, learned how to fix a flat tire, and even had their hair styled! While many parents cannot volunteer their services on a regular basis, if they are asked to come and tell what they do for a living, they usually will. These visits benefit the school, the parent, and the child.

Supporting Shared Decision Making

Although the school and the home share the responsibility for student learning and development, each performs some functions separately. Traditionally, school decision making has been solely the domain of the school system, and "interference" from parents was neither solicited nor welcomed. This model resembles what Epstein (1990) calls "a division of labor that pulls the spheres of school and family influences and responsibilities apart, decreasing overlap and restricting interactions between parents and teachers" (p. 104). In contrast, Epstein advocates a "combination of labor that pushes the spheres of family and school influence together," resulting in what she calls "school-like families'" and "family-like schools" (p. 104). A "school-like family" is created when teachers enlist parents as partners in their children's education. Similarly, a "family-like school" results when teachers, in an effort to "teach the whole child," pay attention to each student's home life, self-concept, aspirations, social skills, and talents.

In their efforts to improve, most schools can do more to enlist the help of parents and community members. When parents understand and help plan and implement new programs and procedures, they are much more likely to be supportive. This is certainly true in the move toward whole language. As we discussed in chapter three, whole language can be explained satisfactorily to most individuals because it makes sense. However, because it represents a change it does need to be thoroughly explained. Parents and community members need to understand *why* elementary school students no longer need to complete vast numbers of worksheets. And they need to understand and support the school's acquisition of children's literature and other necessary materials. They also need the chance to discuss the literature that the students will be reading and the reasons for the selection of each piece.

Similarly, parents need to understand that their children will be involved in extended projects that require sustained interest and effort rather than in the short and often isolated assignments that are the norm in a traditional program. And they need to be able to discuss the types of themes their children will study and the projects students will carry out.

At Oakwood, getting parents involved in decision making meant changing not only staff attitudes but also parents' perceptions of their own role. To this end, the Oakwood staff spent a great deal of time rethinking past practices. For example, after much discussion they decided to change the "Meet the Teacher Night" scheduled each September to a "Meet the

Parent Night." At first parents did not feel comfortable enough to exchange ideas freely, so teachers worked hard to create a relaxed atmosphere that encouraged parents to participate. Now the chairs are arranged in circles, and the children are invited to attend the meeting with their parents. Whereas this had traditionally been a time for teachers to explain the program to parents, teachers now first ask the parents to share their knowledge of their child's interests and feelings, strengths and weaknesses. Then teachers ask the

Figure 5.7

SURVEY

Name _____

Date _____

Grade _____

MY CHILD AS A WRITER
(An Observation Guide for Parents)

Indicate your observation of your child's writing in the following areas. Use a scale of 1 (shows little interest and ability) to 5 (shows intense interest and performance).* Make comments where appropriate.

1. MY CHILD VOLUNTARILY ENGAGES IN INDEPENDENT WRITING/DRAWING ACTIVITY. _____

2. MY CHILD LIKES TO TALK ABOUT/DISPLAY HIS/HER WRITING/DRAWING. _____

3. MY CHILD USES WRITING TO SEND MESSAGES TO OTHERS. _____

4. MY CHILD WILL TRY OUT NEW LETTERS/WORDS OR FORMS OF WRITING ON HIS/HER OWN. _____

5. OTHERS ARE INCREASINGLY ABLE TO READ WHAT MY CHILD WRITES. _____

6. MY CHILD USUALLY LIKES TO WRITE ABOUT _____

COMMENTS OR QUESTIONS:

_____

_____

_____

* (NOTE THAT YOU MAY OR MAY NOT WISH TO USE A NUMERICAL SCALE.)
INTENDED FOR USE AT A K-1 LEVEL.

---

parents to work with their children in filling out various surveys (figure 5.7). These are collected and discussed. Teachers then ask the parents what the school can do to improve communication, help with homework, and so forth. When teachers show parents that they want and value their suggestions, parents respond in a positive and open manner. They are also more comfortable voicing their opinions and questions.

Some schools have restructured the parent-teacher conference, another traditional activity, in order to promote a feeling of partnership. At these meetings teachers formerly explained the grading system and individual children's standing in the class. Now these meetings place greater emphasis on including the parent in the assessment process and in the community of learners. The teacher spends more time listening to the parent and encouraging involvement at home.

Sample Parent-Teacher Conference 1

Teacher: I see that Mark will do the reading that is part of his literature study, but I do not see him becoming an independent reader. Do you see him finding reading materials on his own outside of the classroom?

Parent: No. Other than the books that he reads for class, he hasn't been much of a reader.

Teacher: Do you have any suggestions as to how we could encourage him to seek out reading for information and for recreation?

Parent: Sometimes he and his father can get into a conversation about what is on the sports page. Perhaps we could promote that.

Teacher: Good idea! I should be able to locate some sports stories that he may be interested in reading during our daily sustained silent reading time.

Sample Parent-Teacher Conference 2

Teacher: Susan has wonderful ideas and uses excellent vocabulary in oral communication but is reluctant to express herself in writing. I'd like for her to be more of a risk taker when it comes to writing what she is really thinking. She seems to want the spelling to be perfect, so she only uses words that she knows she can spell. Have you noticed this, too?

Parent: I help her with her spelling at home. Sometimes she wants words that are really too hard for her. Should I help her or not?

Teacher: Reassure her that you are willing to help, but tell her that you want her to go ahead and write what she wants to say first. I'll do the same. We do not want to frustrate her, but she needs to know that her thoughts are the most important thing about writing.

During each conference teacher and parents examine the child's portfolio. Portfolio assessment lends itself to parental involvement in a way that browsing through a traditional stack of workbook pages simply does not. The teacher asks parents their opinions about what they see as their child's strengths and weaknesses. The parents' assessment of the child's work helps the teacher and also gives the parent special knowledge about their child and her or his capabilities. Parents come to view their role in the conference as an important part of their child's education.

Providing Support and Sustenance

In order to maintain a healthy relationship between school and parents, the school, school system administrators, and school board must provide the necessary support. Such support may include: (1) scheduling inservice opportunities directed generally at helping teachers work with parents and specifically at helping teachers conduct effective parent-teacher conferences and parent education workshops; (2) supporting the parent-teacher organization; (3) making parents, community members, and other visitors welcome in the school; and (4) asking parents and community members to serve on decision-making councils and advisory groups.

The school system and school leaders also need to conduct a parent and community survey to identify strengths and needs in the areas of home-school communication, parent education, and public relations. Additionally, most schools find it especially helpful if both a parent and a teacher serve as co-chairs of a planning group to review areas of need and make recommendations about parent-community involvement. It would also be helpful to have one or two nonparental community members serve on this committee. The administrators can help this group by coordinating meeting times and places and by being accessible during the meetings. Through their sincere interest in and appreciation of the activities conducted by these individuals, the system and school leaders demonstrate their support.

The administrators' primary function in building a strong three-way partnership is to foster trust in the school, in the faculty, and in the administration. This trust can only be established when the administrators truly believe that parent and community involvement is one of the most important aspects of any school. This belief must be clearly shown by a school faculty and administration whose day-to-day operations reflect the principles described in this chapter for creating effective and lasting partnerships.

It is imperative that we as educators consider carefully the advantages of parent empowerment. While we readily admit that many more students would be successful if their families were closely involved in a home-school partnership, we must first agree on the responsibilities that each partner will fulfill. When parents and community members are empowered as valuable, contributing partners in the educational process, everyone benefits.

References:

– **Bauch, P. A.** (1988). Is parent involvement different in private schools? *Education Horizons, 66(2),* 78–82.

– **Berger, E. H.** (1981). *Parents as partners in education.* St. Louis, MO: C. V. Mosby.

– **Boyer, E. L.** (1991). *Ready to learn: A mandate for the nation.* The Carnegie Foundation for the Advancement of Teaching. Lawrenceville, NJ: Princeton University Press.

– **Chrispeels, J. H.** (1991). District leadership in parent involvement. *Phi Delta Kappan, 72(5),* 367–371.

– **Cochran, M., & Henderson, C. R.** (1987). Family matters: Evaluation of the parental empowerment program. In Henderson, A. (Ed.), *The evidence continues to grow* (pp. 25–26). Columbia, MD: National Committee for Citizens in Education.

– **Dauber, S. L., & Epstein, J. L.** (1989, March). Parents' attitudes and practices of involvement in inner-city elementary and middle schools. Paper presented at the annual meeting of the American Educational Research Association, San Francisco.

– **Dembo, M., Sweitzer, M., & Lauritzen, P.** (1985). An evaluation of group parent education: Behavioral, PET and adlerian programs. *Review of Educational Research, 55(2),* 155–200.

– **Dornbusch, S. M., & Ritter, P. L.** (1988). Parents of high school students: A neglected resource. *Educational Horizons, 66,* 75–77.

– **Dulaney, K.** (1987). A comprehensive approach for parent and community involvement. *Illinois School Journal,* pp. 42–48. Chicago: Chicago State University.

– **Elam, S. M., Rose, L. C., & Gallup, A. M.** (1991). The 23rd annual Gallup poll of the public's attitudes toward the public schools. *Phi Delta Kappan, 73(1),* 41–56.

– **Epstein, J. L.** (1985). A question of merit: Principals' and parents' evaluations of teachers. *Educational Researcher, 14(7),* 3–10.

– **Epstein, J. L.** (1986). Parents' reactions to teacher practices of parent involvement. *The Elementary School Journal, 86(3),* 277–294.

– **Epstein, J. L.** (1987). Parent involvement: What research says to administrators. *Education and Urban Society, 19(2),* 119–136.

– **Epstein, J. L.** (1988). How do we improve programs in parent involvement? *Educational Horizons, 66(2),* 58–59.

– **Epstein, J. L.** (1990). School and family connections: Theory, research, and implications for integrating sociologies of education and family. In D. G. Unger and M. B. Sussman (Eds.), *Families in community settings: Interdisciplinary perspectives* (pp. 99–124). New York: Haworth Press.

– **EQUALS** (1986). *Family math.* Berkeley: University of California.

– **Henderson, A.** (1987). *The evidence continues to grow: Parent involvement improves student achievement.* Columbia, MD: National Committee for Citizens in Education.

– **Henderson, A. T., Marburger, C. L., & Ooms, T.** (1986). *Beyond the bake sale: An educator's guide to working with parents.* Columbia, MD: National Committee for Citizens in Education.

– **Moles, O. C.** (1987).Who wants parent involvement? *Education and Urban Society, 19(2),* 137–145.

– **Northwest EQUALS,** (1988). *Family science.* Portland, OR: Portland State University.

– **Powell, D. R.** (1986, March). Parent education and support programs. *Young Children,* pp. 7–53.

Saying Yes to Accountability: The Assessment and Evaluation of Learning

A Note from Elizabeth . . .

A superintendent from a school outside St. Louis asked to visit with me. A group of teachers from his district had attended a workshop conducted by members of our Oakwood School faculty. I was in the process of describing some of the major components of our curriculum when he stopped me and asked what I could show him that could be considered evidence of the effectiveness of our approach. I asked him to come back after lunch. Thirty minutes later I had a wonderful collection of artifacts—all gathered from one first-grade classroom. He was impressed . . . and so was I! The one teacher I had time to visit with during that lunch break had such a wonderful wealth of information . . . right at her fingertips! Such convincing assessment data would never have been so readily available had this teacher been teaching in a traditional program.

A Brief Look at a Traditional Approach to Assessment

Let's think for a moment about the kinds of assessment information we might find in a traditional classroom. Because traditional assessment calls for subtracting points from our standard of 100 percent, the teacher in this classroom would undoubtedly have a grade book in which she or he records percentages earned on a number of objectives measures, such as weekly spelling tests, end-of-level basal tests, and skill drills. We might also find student folders containing a few graded worksheets or workbook pages, standardized test booklets, and perhaps a couple of teacher-made tests.

Clearly, when we think of assessment in a traditional classroom, the emphasis is on documenting student learning by examining specific products. This is most commonly done through formal and informal tests—tests that yield summative rather than formative evaluative information. In an effort to be "objective" in their grading, traditional teachers devalue more subjective means of assessment such as teacher observation, checklists, and anecdotal records in favor of discrete, finite, paper-and-pencil tasks to which a numerical score can be assigned.

This overreliance on so-called "objective" measures of student progress persists in most traditional classrooms, despite a growing number of studies that continue to reveal the negative impact of tests (Shepard, 1988; Brown, 1989; Cannell, 1988; Hiebert & Calfee, 1992) and that caution against the increasing trend to let test content drive curriculum and instruction planning. These studies have, in turn, prompted at least two professional educational organizations to recommend a ban against standardized testing—at least in the primary years. In a position paper titled "On Standardized Testing," the Association for Childhood Education International states, "We now believe firmly that no standardized testing should occur in the preschool and K-2 years. Further, we question seriously the need for testing every child in the remainder of the elementary years" (p. 137).

Similarly, according to Constance Kamii and Mieko Kamii, editors of *Achievement Testing in the Early Grades: The Games Grown-ups Play* (NAEYC, 1990):

> The authors of this book are calling for a halt to achievement testing in grades K-2 for two reasons: These tests are not valid measures of children's learning or of teachers' accountability, and the pressure for higher test scores is resulting in classroom practices that are harmful to young children's development. (p. 15).

They exhort readers to call a halt to achievement testing in grades K-2 and to "rethink not only assessment procedures but also our educational goals and methods of teaching" (p. 15).

Districts, schools, and classrooms whose educational goals do not include, for example, critical, independent thinking or interest in further learning will probably omit these goals and their corresponding objectives from the overall plan for assessment and evaluation. As we pointed out in chapter 1, the traditional model of education is a transmission model where part-to-whole learning is emphasized. Thus, our model for assessing student progress and evaluating programs has traditionally followed suit, requiring children to demonstrate mastery of the various isolated knowledge, skills, and attitudes that make up a particular curricular area. As a result of this transmission model of assessment, we see a diminishing curriculum where higher-order thinking skills, exploration of real-world materials, and authentic literacy tasks are being supplanted by an increasing number of worksheets, workbooks, and lower-level "skills"—all in an effort to "raise test scores."

When we look at the concepts that support assessment in a whole language classroom, traditional ideas regarding the hows and whys of assessment seem totally inadequate. A new view of assessment, then, must accompany our new view of schooling.

Linking Assessment and Instruction in the Whole Language Classroom

As teachers and administrators move toward a whole language philosophy of education, one of the greatest challenges they face is that of devising authentic and trustworthy assessment that reflects the real literacy and learning of their students (Lamme & Hysmith, 1991). As Weaver (1992) points out, in a whole language classroom, "whatever the particular means, assessment data is gathered primarily while the learner is engaged in authentic literacy and/or learning experiences, not in an isolated test situation" (p. 13).

Principles that guide assessment in a whole language classroom are basically the same principles that guide curriculum planning. First of all, students are actively engaged in numerous meaningful, real-life learning experiences that require them to integrate a variety of knowledge, skills, and attitudes. As an integral part of each learning experience, assessment is both ongoing and continuous and allows for self-evaluation, peer evaluation, and teacher evaluation. This assessment information becomes the basis for decisions about the kinds of future learning experiences that need to occur. Finally, assessment seeks to chart the accomplishments of each individual learner in terms of his or her own past accomplishments rather than to compare learners by means of external criteria or norms (Weaver, 1992).

When assessment and curriculum are seen as both integral and integrated components of the teaching/learning process, marvelous things begin to happen in a school. Not only do teachers become more tolerant of children whose development is not "on grade level," but also the children themselves gain self-confidence as readers, writers, and learners. Additionally, as researchers Johnston, Weiss, and Afflerbach (1989) found, teachers used more innovative curriculum materials, such as children's literature and other trade books, and developed compatible assessment methods to match their curriculum when they were employed in districts where external mandates regarding instruction and assessment had been removed.

As a result of integrating assessment and curriculum, both teachers and students begin to view reading and writing as *processes*. This is important for at least two reasons. One, when we are engaged in a *process* rather than in the creation of a *product,* we assume that we will make mistakes and that we will work to correct them. Also, we are more apt to consciously apply strategies that will help us perform our task and to look for new strategies that will help us when we encounter a problem.In a whole language classroom, the process the children use as they read and write—the strategies they employ—are continually observed and assessed by the teacher. The teacher uses this assessment information to plan instruction that will be immediately useful to the students, who, in turn, are well motivated because they know that what they are learning will help them complete a meaningful and important task.

When reading is viewed as a process of constructing or building meaning based on the words themselves, the background experiences the reader brings to reading, and the purpose for reading (Anderson, Hiebert, Scott, & Wilkinson, 1985), the reader naturally assumes that there may be words that he or she does not understand or know how to pronounce. Good readers constantly monitor, or self-evaluate, their comprehension. They know what to do when they come to a word that they do not know. They have strategies that they can consciously employ to help them decode words that are "strange" in either form or meaning. Similarly, good readers know that they have to adjust their rate of reading to suit the material and their purpose for reading, that they may have to reread parts of the material to clarify the author's meaning, and that they will probably have to stop periodically to summarize what they have read thus far and predict what will come next. Good readers also pause in their reading to ask themselves questions about the material. For example, in a factual piece on the training of a knight in tenth-century England, Sarah read that the young boys were taken from their homes at about the age of seven. Sarah wondered why they had to leave their homes instead of commuting to school as children do today. After reading that the boys were called pages, Sarah asked herself if this is why the students who work in the state capitol building are called pages. As she read about the many duties of pages, she wondered if they attended class to learn subjects like reading, writing, arithmetic, and history.

In a whole language classroom, the teacher models reading as a meaning-getting process, and she or he helps the children learn to consciously apply strategies that good readers, like Sarah, use routinely. Assessment is a continuous part of this process as the teacher observes, listens to, and talks with the reader *during* an authentic reading task. The teacher then uses this information to plan instruction that is specific to each child' needs. In a traditional classroom, reading is more likely to be viewed as a product. The emphasis, then, in assessment is on word-perfect oral reading, correctly answering the questions on a worksheet or posed by the teacher, and responding correctly to various kinds of subskill tasks such as those typically found in most basal reader workbooks—finding the main idea, matching definitions and vocabulary terms, and sequencing events.

Like reading, writing in a whole language classroom is also seen as a process of constructing meaning (Tierney & Pearson, 1984). The writer can use a range of strategies in the planning or prewriting stage of the writing process. Good writers know how to select and narrow a topic, as well as how to assess what they know about the topic and whether or not they will need additional information. They are learning to use library and research skills and also to gather primary-source data through interviews and other appropriate means. They can create written notes, outlines, and webs to help them organize their information. In the drafting stage of the process, writers know that they do not have to stop writing when they want to use a word they do not know how to spell. Likewise, they know that they will have ample opportunity to improve both the content and form of their writing during the revising and editing stages of the writing process. The teacher oversees every stage of this process; thus ongoing assessment is an integral part of a process approach to writing.

Children whom the teacher observes having difficulty during a particular stage are guided to recognize and develop the skills or strategies they need at that time. Through keen observation the teacher is able to tailor her or his instruction to each learner, thus enabling the students to develop those skills and strategies they most need.

For example, Joseph, a fifth-grade student, has written a wonderful "Just So" story in the style of Rudyard Kipling. In his story he explains how the rainbow came to be. During a final editing conference the teacher, at three different points in the story, has to ask Joseph to identify which character is speaking. Although Joseph is always able to clarify the confusion for his teacher, she asks him how he thinks his readers will solve this problem, since he will not be available. As the teacher helps Joseph look at his story from a reader's perspective, he recognizes a problem for which he isn't quite sure of the solution. The teacher suggests that he look to see how other authors have handled similar situations. After examining one or two books, Joseph realizes that quotation marks and paragraphing are two ways authors show when various characters are speaking.

Ken Goodman tells us that we learn from our errors (1969). Similarly, teachers learn from their pupils' errors. Carol Davis, a first-grade teacher at Oakwood School who understands this concept of assessment, gives a spelling test to her class in September. She calls out twenty words for the children to spell. After collecting the papers, Carol sets up individual recordkeeping sheets for each child (see figure 6.1). The first column lists the words Carol included in the spelling test. In the second column she writes the date and then the child's

Figure 6.1

SPELLING ASSESSMENT RECORD

Name	10-17-91	12-9-91				
1. rag	rak	rag				
2. hit	hat	hepd				
3. den	dn	den				
4. bus	bs	bas				
5. six	sk	sea				
6. name	nain	nma				
7 grass	gras	gae				
8. drive	dri	iagv				
9. shopping	sph	sapen				
10. kite	kit	kit				
11. truck	trk	traic				
12. doctor	dt	dakr				
13. pink	pk	peck				
14. seven	sin	safn				
15. everything	efria	afirfa				
16. silly	sele	sele				
17. skating	skate	saten				
18. next	nest	nasa				
19. flower	flr	flor				
20. water	wtr	wad				

Notes: _____

_____

_____

_____

_____

_____

_____

_____

_____

_____

spelling for each word. Carol will use the other columns to keep track of the child's performance on periodic retests of the same words.

As might be expected, very few children are able to spell the words conventionally; however, Carol now has a standard by which to judge each child's growth in spelling, and she also has a great deal of assessment information that can help her plan the curriculum. Carol analyzes each child's spellings, noting how he or she applies spelling strategies, letter-sound relationships, and generalizations. For example, she notices that many children use only initial consonants. These children will benefit from seeing many words both in books and in the environment and from group dictation exercises in which she will model listening for final consonant and for vowel sounds. Carol also notices that other children are using some phonetic spellings. She will be able to assess which letter-sound relationships these children have already mastered. Still other children are overgeneralizing various phonetic "rules." For example, some spell the word *bright* as *brite*. This spelling lets her know that the child understands and can apply the "final *e*" phonic generalization, even though it is not appropriate in this particular instance.

It is highly unlikely that a teacher in a traditional first-grade classroom would give a spelling test at the start of the school year. This is largely because spelling is not routinely taught during the first semester of first grade. However, if a test *were* given, the teacher in a traditional classroom probably would simply record a numerical rating, an "F," or possibly a "U," for each child's pretest score. The whole language teacher, like Carol, would analyze the errors, or miscues, and then use this information to plan instruction that will help each child move toward conventional spelling.

The emphasis on *process-oriented* assessment does not, however, preclude having any *product-oriented* assessment. Products, such as a student's oral reading during a Reader's Theater or a report on medieval knights, yield important assessment information. Yet they give us only a part of the total picture.

As assessment and curriculum become more and more entwined, the classroom becomes more and more a "community of learners" (Hansen, 1987) where not only reading and writing abilities but also self-concepts *flourish*. In the classroom communities at Oakwood, we no longer celebrate just the "A." We celebrate all our achievements, even those that fall short of perfection. We have learned to share not only our successes but also our weaknesses so that we can truly accept children as they are and help them grow. It is important to note that we share this concept in common with our students' parents. Childrearing, whether in school or in the home, becomes much less frustrating when we expect and reward *growth* rather than *perfection*. In a whole language school every step along that path is encouraged, recognized, and praised.

Teachers as Professional Observers

When Yetta Goodman shared her concept of assessment in "Kid-watching" (1978), she gave every teacher permission to judge what children were learning in the classroom and to trust that judgment as a valuable tool in curriculum planning. Application of the skill that is being taught is the true test of mastery. This is true whether we are talking about driving an automobile, performing a high-dive, or using quotation marks appropriately. When teachers are told that they are better judges of their students than any standardized test or worksheet, they take this responsibility seriously. In so doing, they grow as professionals. They develop both the confidence and the skills that allow them to become researchers in their own classrooms. They formulate clear mental pictures of the goals that each child is capable of reaching, and they develop assessment tools and record-keeping procedures that will help them keep track of each child's progress toward those goals.

Teachers often need a great deal of support from administrators as they develop their "kidwatching" skills. Like any new endeavor, recording observational information requires practice. It also requires time! As teachers develop and pilot various kinds of checklists, anecdotal record forms, and teacher logbooks, they struggle with time management. However time-consuming this might be, as far as we are concerned it is a necessary and unavoidable part of implementing assessment procedures that are compatible with a whole language philosophy of learning.

In spite of teachers' frequent complaints about unavoidable circumstances such as school assemblies and field trips that cause them to fall behind in collecting assessment information, *all* teachers we know who have assumed the role of "kidwatcher" or "professional observer" readily agree that they are more in tune with what students can and cannot yet do and are infinitely more qualified to judge pupil progress than they were in previous years when they assumed more of a role of "teacher as testgiver." As teachers work to sharpen their observation and notetaking skills, they often feel overwhelmed by the sheer magnitude of the job of assessing every child in the class. The natural tendency is for teachers to say, "I give up! I can't do it!" when they find themselves falling behind the goals they have set for themselves for observing and conferencing with students. These goals are often too high, particularly when a teacher is trying out new assessment procedures. Administrators can help teachers be more realistic in their goals for the number of observations recorded and conferences held. In the early stages of a new assessment strategy, it might be possible for the administrator to arrange for teaching aides or classroom volunteers to be on hand while the teacher meets with individuals and small groups of students. Finding time to observe and talk with students is not, however, as difficult as it might first appear. It is important to keep in mind the structure of a whole language classroom, where independent and collaborative learning are highly valued. Additionally, as we move away from the "transmission" model of education discussed in chapter 1, we free the teacher to *facilitate* rather than *direct* learning. Teacher observation and conferencing is a critical component in facilitating the learning process.

The Importance of Self-Evaluation

Just as teachers must learn to trust their own ability to observe and document students' progress, so must they come to regard children's opinions of themselves as valuable and necessary sources of assessment information. The learner as self-evaluator is a key player in a whole language classroom. As teachers and children become comfortable with their complementary roles as both evaluator and learner, the classroom community is both enhanced and enriched.

Children become very conscious of teachers' observation of their progress, not just on tests but also on their application of the skills they have been learning. It is not uncommon for a child to say to the teacher during a literature discussion, "Did you hear me compare and contrast characters?" or "I have found an example of cause and effect in this story."

Mary, a first-grader, shared her story with the principal. As she read she pointed out where she had used commas in the right places, and she asked the principal to tell the teacher to check off commas in the teacher's assessment notebook. This is a common occurrence in many whole language classrooms where children are encouraged to evaluate their own ability to apply the knowledge, skills, and attitudes that they are acquiring.

Very rarely are children in a traditional classroom asked to assess themselves. Yet if we want children to take responsibility for their learning, we must teach them how to engage in conscious and ongoing reflection and self-evaluation. This process helps children see themselves as readers and writers. They become aware of what they know and of skills they have and are able to apply and that they still need to develop.

In a traditional classroom we assess children by comparing them with other children. Conversely, in a whole language classroom, the teacher assesses children in terms of their growth as readers, writers, mathematicians, scientists, musicians, artists, and so on. Children come to see growth as a comparison with themselves. They ask, "What do I know now, or what can I do now, that I did not know or could not do before?"

The teachers we work with have had to learn to value children's views of themselves and to help children set goals for future learning. All of these pieces of information become important parts of an assessment plan.

Oakwood's Assessment Plan

The assessment information I shared with the superintendent who was visiting our district was from a first-grade teacher's room. I could just as easily have gathered these artifacts from any of our classrooms, for although each teacher does have some individual preferences and strategies for assessment, the school staff as a whole has agreed on some very important functions for our assessment. While we are happy to share some of the assessment tools and strategies that work for us, we offer these only as examples of the many ways a school staff or an individual teacher might go about obtaining and using assessment information. Like us, you too will need to adapt these tools and strategies to fit your particular situation—your teachers, students, and parents. While working out one's own individual assessment plan is, without a doubt, extremely time-consuming, it is time well spent. As whole language teachers will readily admit, assessing and recording pupil progress in a whole language classroom is not easy. It is only by actually using these techniques that we begin to feel more comfortable with ourselves as professional observers.

FUNCTION ONE:
LANGUAGE MUST BE ASSESSED IN REAL SITUATIONS

In a whole language classroom where application of specific skills and strategies for learning is the criterion for mastery, teachers must devise ways to assess whether or not students *can* and *do* apply these important elements *while they are doing a meaningful, purposeful task.* For example, Melanie, a fourth-grader in Penny Strube's classroom, is sharing an entry in her literature log. In it she wrote that Helen Keller's handicap caused her to be a problem child. Mrs. Strube notes that Melanie is able to detect cause and effect relationships as she reads. In her analysis of Helen Keller's character, Melanie also contrasted Helen's childhood with her adulthood. Again, Mrs. Strube notes that Melanie can compare and contrast character traits and recognize the ways a particular character changed.

FUNCTION TWO: ASSESSMENT MUST INFORM TEACHING

As noted earlier in the chapter, assessment and instruction go hand in hand in a whole language classroom. Assessment tools and strategies are not used only at the end of particular lesson, unit, project, grading period, or school year. Rather, continuous and ongoing assessment of language and literacy in real learning situations is the foundation of our everyday instructional practices.

Stephen, a first-grader, does not need instruction on the sound that *ph* makes. He mastered this concept early when he learned to write his name. Similarly, students who can correctly write words with *ing* and *ed* do not need instruction on these word endings, nor do they need to demonstrate this ability on a worksheet or test. Their own spontaneous writing shows their mastery of this skill.

When assessment informs instruction, a teacher does not introduce a skill to a group of students of whom some are already using the skill and some are not yet ready to use it. Rather, she or he works with individuals or small groups who have not mastered a particular skill but who have a purpose for using it. When handled in this manner, the entire instructional process becomes very efficient.

FUNCTION THREE: CHILDREN ARE ASSESSED USING CLEAR INDICATORS THAT ARE APPROPRIATE FOR EACH CHILD

Assessment must be made on an individual basis. The teacher should expect children at different levels of development to demonstrate different skills. For example, while one child may be asked to use end marks or capital letters, another child may be expected to use quotation marks and commas. The degree to which each child can demonstrate these skills determines the score or grade he or she earns for that part of the overall assignment or project. Teachers often assign a rating to each component or skill, most often when the student and teacher are conferring about a particular project or piece of writing. If a first-grade student had fulfilled the requirement that all of the words be separated by spaces, then he or she would receive the highest rating for that particular skill.

This assessment strategy helps children develop good independent work habits. The few minutes it takes the teacher to determine with the child what a particular piece of work needs and the teacher's subsequent explanation, demonstration, or minilesson ensure that the child receives the right kind of instruction at the right time, in the right amount, and at the right level.

FUNCTION FOUR: ASSESSMENT MUST GUIDE THE CHILD

We have already discussed how assessment guides instruction. Assessment must also guide the child. In a whole language classroom, the children are intricately involved in the assessment process; therefore, "surprises" in assessment and/or grading should never occur. The teacher encourages the child's involvement in a number of ways, such as by providing for learner self-assessment, peer conferencing and assessment, and student/teacher conferencing and assessment. When the teacher prepares an evaluation sheet of a rough draft, the child has an opportunity to provide input, ask questions, and review with the teacher what needs to be done. Through this process, the child becomes empowered as an active participant in her or his own learning and in the assessment of that learning.

FUNCTION FIVE: ASSESSMENT MUST INCLUDE AN OPPORTUNITY FOR STUDENT SELF-ASSESSMENT

In many traditional classrooms children's work is judged only by the teacher. Children are told how well they perform as readers, writers, and mathematicians. They are told how well they listen and speak and how skilled they are at remembering and applying content-area knowledge. Many times children perform only well enough to earn an acceptable grade. The reward is so extrinsic that children of high ability often put very little effort into their work. However, when the teacher begins to share the responsibilities of assessment with the children, they begin to gain insights into themselves as readers, writers, mathematicians, speakers, listeners, and so forth. They begin to set and to strive for goals that will please themselves rather than just the teacher.

Self-evaluation takes many forms at Oakwood. Many teachers use checklists at the conclusion of a literature study group. Even first-grade children can assume responsibility for completing the form that Carol Davis and Suzanne Gottman developed to use with their literature units (see figure 6.2). Or teachers may include, on an essay exam, for example, a section where students assess their individual contributions to the theme study. At other times teachers may include self-assessment as a part of the evaluation sheet for a particular assignment or project, asking children to rate themselves on a number of criteria. In the example shown in figure 6.3, the students in Paula Ingebretson's second-grade class are asked to write about what they especially liked about their report, what they think would have improved their report, two specific facts or skills that they learned from

Figure 6.2

LITERATURE GROUP SELF-EVALUATION FORM

Name _____

Date _____

Book _____

_____ 1. I did my best in my literature log.

_____ 2. I read my book at home every night.

_____ 3. I discussed in my literature group.

_____ 4. I did my best on my project.

Great   OK   Need to Work

Figure 6.3

EVALUATION REPORT

Date _____

Name _____

Evaluation on _____ Report

Topic _____

What I liked best:

What I think would have improved the report:

I learned:

I learned:

I would like to learn:

Figure 6.4

PUBLISHING JOURNEY
Paula Ingebratson, Grade 1

Name _____ Date _____

Title _____

Self:

    Read over to myself. _____

    Add or change something. _____

    Edit for spelling. _____

    Edit for punctuation. _____

Peer:

    Read to _____.

    Add or change something. _____

    Edit for spelling. _____

    Edit for punctuation. _____

Teacher:

    Conference Box 1 _____

    Read to teacher. _____

    Add or change something. _____

    Edit for spelling. _____

    Conference Box 2 _____

    Meet with teacher. _____

    Recopy _____

Publishing Box _____

Illustrations Box _____

Author's Chair _____ Date _____

---

doing the project, and what they would like to learn more about.

Students in whole language classrooms assess their peers as well as themselves. Most classrooms use some form of the author's chair (Graves & Hansen, 1987), a peer-conferencing strategy wherein pupils read their stories and reports to a group of classmates. The classmates perform a valuable service for the student author when they provide "audience feedback" about the piece. In addition, some teachers ask students to write their assessments of a peer's work. The "Publishing Journey" sheet developed by Paula Ingebretson (see figure 6.4) is divided into sections for self-assessment, peer assessment, and teacher assessment.

When students are consistently asked to assess themselves, the responsibility for learning begins to shift from teacher to student. Holding children responsible for participating in the assessment process makes them more aware of skills and concepts. Teachers who give children this responsibility see it as a major contributor to the developing sense of community in the classroom. Self-evaluation becomes an attitude that develops in a democratic classroom. It is the natural outcome of the trust that teachers give to children.

FUNCTION SIX:
READING AND WRITING ARE ASSESSED AS PROCESSES

Because a whole language teacher views reading and writing as processes, she or he collects information at every stage of the process. At Oakwood, the primary means of collecting information about the reading process is the Reading Miscue Inventory (1972), which is primarily a method of recording and analyzing a child's oral reading strategies. Although special training is recommended, a teacher can easily become proficient at using this tool and can accurately assess a student's strengths and weaknesses in decoding and comprehension strategies.

Assessment of written language must also reflect what we know about writing as a process; therefore, teachers observe and analyze children's abilities to use prewriting strategies such as brainstorming, webbing, outlining, interviewing, and notetaking. While assessing a rough draft the teacher may look at the child's ability to organize ideas and thoughts into a coherent piece of writing rather than at spelling and punctuation, as the good writer knows that the latter skills are best addressed during the editing stage of the writing process.

While assessing the revising stage, the teacher will evaluate the student's ability to improve the content of the piece by reworking the rough draft. Primarily, the teacher will assess the student's ability to evaluate and change the content of her or his writing through such strategies as rereading the piece and conferencing with peers and/or the teacher to gain insights into an audience's response to it. In the editing stage the teacher pays attention to the mechanics of grammar, punctuation, and spelling as the author prepares a piece of writing to be published and shared.

A teacher might assess a student's ability to edit a piece of writing by asking the student to circle all of the words that he or she *thinks* might be misspelled. Another teacher might have a student underline the topic sentence in each paragraph of an expository essay or use different-colored pens to mark where each character in a story begins and ends speaking.

Finally, during the sharing stage of the writing process the teacher might assess a student's ability to choose a good way to publish her or his writing. This may involve bookmaking activities, where the student types or rewrites the text, provides illustrations if appropriate, and binds the book. Assessing this final stage in the writing process might also include evaluating students' effectiveness at reading their completed writings to their classmates.

FUNCTION SEVEN:
ASSESSMENT HELPS PARENTS UNDERSTAND
THE ONGOING DEVELOPMENT OF THEIR CHILD

The goals of home-school communication are three-fold. First of all, teachers want to help parents encourage and promote their child's learning. Teachers do this by giving parents helpful information about the benefits of reading to their children, talking with them, and listening to them as they read, as well as by sharing specific tips about their child throughout the school year.

Secondly, teachers want to convey to parents the specific behaviors and skills that they look for while assessing children. For example, can the child use the context of the sentence to figure out the pronunciation and meaning of an unfamiliar word? By familiarizing parents with the strategies teachers look for, they are helping parents recognize the particular strengths and needs of their children.

Finally, it is important to keep parents well informed about the status of the long-range independent projects that many whole language teachers stress. This means informing parents about the stages of a particular project and giving them regular updates about the child's progress.

Like many districts, ours is still bound by the constraints of a very traditional reporting system that includes a districtwide grade card. Because of this, we take very seriously our responsibility to keep parents well informed through both the information we send home and our regular parent-teacher conferences. We have found that the teachers' observation notes and checklists and samples of each child's work are extremely valuable during parent-teacher conferences. Additionally, we regularly send some of this information home between conferences. For example, Carol Davis and Suzanne Gottman, two first-grade teachers at Oakwood, send home quarterly evaluation sheets (see figures 6.5, 6.6, and 6.7) in an effort to inform parents of their child's progress in reading, mathematics, and spelling. The parents sign and return the bottom portion of each sheet, which also includes a place for comments.

To supplement the various projects and papers that routinely are sent home, parents can also take home videotapes showing children sharing projects or reports with their peers. Children also read into a tape recorder every month, and the tapes, which teachers use to assess oral reading, are shared with parents.

Journals of children's daily writing are also sent home. These provide a wonderful record of growth, even of a very young child or a child who is

Figure 6.5

THIRD QUARTER READING EVALUATION

STUDENT_____DATE_____

Carol Davis/Suzanne Gottman, First Grade teachers, Oakwood School

Listed below are the objectives/skills for Reading this quarter. A check indicates that your child has mastered this skill, based on his/her daily progress.

_____ 1. Participates in Shared Reading. (Big Book)

_____ 2. Attentive during Shared Reading.

_____ 3. Asks meaningful questions during Twenty Questions.

_____ 4. Able to read (chorally) Twenty Questions from chart.

_____ 5. Attentive for weekly poems.

_____ 6. Able to read weekly poems with group.

_____ 7. Leads week's poems for class.

_____ 8. Attends to print in literature book.

_____ 9. Does his/her best work in literature log.

_____10. Shares ideas during literature.

_____11. Self-evaluates progress honestly for literature group.

_____12. Returns literature book daily. (responsibility)

_____13. Recognizes vocabulary in literature book.

_____14. Does his/her best work on literature project.

_____15. Able to sequence literature story.

_____16. Knows meaning of vocabulary in literature book.

_____17. Able to read independently during DEAR time.

_____18. Able to write meaningful stories for Writer's Workshop.

_____19. Able to read own story for Writer's Workshop.

_____20. Able to make meaningful predictions about events
         of a story using a variety of reading selections.

_____21. Able to state examples of synonyms.

_____22. Able to state examples of antonyms.

_____23. Able to state Main Idea of a story.

_____24. Able to distinguish between reality and fantasy.

_____25. Recognizes words with long vowels. (a, e, i, o, u)

_____26. Recognizes compound words and knows that a
         compound is made up of two words.

_____27. Able to classify words into groups.
         (bus, car, truck – transportation)

PLEASE SIGN AND RETURN BOTTOM PORTION ONLY!!! THANKS!!!

Parent Signature:_____

Comments (if any)

Figure 6.6

MATH EVALUATION THIRD QUARTER

STUDENT_____DATE_____

Carol Davis/Suzanne Gottman, First Grade teachers, Oakwood School

Listed below are the objectives/skills for Math this quarter. A check indicates that your child has mastered this skill, based on his/her daily progress.

_____ 1. Able to state today's date using calendar.

_____ 2. Able to state number of days we have been in school.

_____ 3. Knows own birthday.

_____ 4. Able to count by 2's to 100.

_____ 5. Able to state days we have been in school in tens and ones.

_____ 6. Able to count by 5's to 100.

_____ 7. Able to count by 10's to 100.

_____ 8. Able to tell date BEFORE today's date.

_____ 9. Able to tell date AFTER today's date.

_____10. Able to count from 1-100.

_____11. Works with numbers on CONCEPT level. (3)

_____12. Works with numbers on CONCEPT level. (4)

_____13. Works with numbers on CONCEPT level. (5)

_____14. Works with numbers on CONCEPT level. (6)

_____15. Works with numbers on CONCEPT level. (7)

_____16. Works with numbers on CONCEPT level. (8)

_____17. Works with numbers on CONCEPT level. (9)

_____18. Recognizes numerals 0-100.

_____19. Able to write numerals 0-100.

_____20. Able to count backwards from 20-0.

_____21. Works with numbers on CONNECTING level. (3)

_____22. Works with numbers on CONNECTING level. (4)

_____23. Works with numbers on CONNECTING level. (5)

_____24. Works with numbers on CONNECTING level. (6)

_____25. Works with numbers on CONNECTING level. (7)

_____26. Works with numbers on CONNECTING level. (8)

_____27. Works with numbers on CONNECTING level. (9)

_____28. Able to tell time to the hour.

_____29. Able to tell time to the half-hour.

PLEASE SIGN AND RETURN BOTTOM PORTION ONLY!!! THANKS!!!

Parent Signature:_____

Comments (if any)

Figure 6.7

SPELLING MID TERM REPORT
THIRD QUARTER

STUDENT_____DATE_____

Carol Davis/Suzanne Gottman, First Grade teachers, Oakwood School

Listed below are the objectives/skills for Spelling this quarter. A check indicates the level where your child performs MOST of the time, based on daily progress.

JOURNAL

_____ Uses conventional spelling 50% or more in daily journal entry.

_____ At least 1/2 of words in journal for each day are conventional spelling.

_____ Daily entry is approaching conventional spelling.

_____ Uses vowels - but either incorrect vowel or incorrect place.

_____ Spells with only beginning, middle and ending sounds.

_____ Spells with beginning and ending sounds.

_____ Spells with beginning sounds only.

_____ Spells with random letters.

_____ Uses pictures to tell story and no words, letters, etc.

_____ Copies words from around room, books, etc.

_____ Makes no attempt to write in journal.

SPELLING TESTS

_____ Spells with conventional spelling.

_____ Spells with beginning, middle and ending sounds with vowel, but incorrect vowel or incorrect place.

_____ Spells with beginning, middle and ending sounds only.

_____ Spells with beginning and ending sounds.

_____ Spells with beginning, ending OR middle sounds.

_____ Makes NO attempt - spells with random letters.

PLEASE SIGN AND RETURN BOTTOM PORTION ONLY!!! THANKS!!!

Parent Signature:_____

Comments (if any)

experiencing a developmental lag. Seeing a child's writing progress from primarily scribbles and mock letters to acceptable English letters is a powerful encouragement to most parents. Carol Davis and Suzanne Gottman use the students' journals to assess spelling. In the quarterly report for spelling that they send home, they indicate the level at which the child most frequently performs each of the listed objectives and skills (see figure 6.7). Most parents readily understand this information because they have read their child's journal entries.

Besides the assessment information that is based on the child's current work, our Oakwood parents appreciate seeing long-term documentation of their child's growth and progress. This documentation consists of the artifacts that teachers collect in an individual *portfolio* for each student. Parents of the fifth-grade children who are graduating from Oakwood are always especially pleased to receive this portfolio of artifacts that illustrate their child's progression through the elementary grades.

Oakwood's Assessment Tools

For the most part, whole language teachers build evaluation into their day-to-day teaching activities. Questioning the validity and usefulness of traditional evaluation tools such as standardized tests or other multiple choice instruments, they rely instead on interaction with the pupils, on observation of pupil performance, and on analysis of pupil behaviors. Since assessment is viewed as an integral part of the curriculum, the tools used by the teachers at Oakwood to collect, analyze, and record pupil progress are also used in instructional and curricular decision making.

THE MONITORING NOTEBOOK

There are many tools that teachers have found helpful in recording children's grasp of specific skills and strategies. One such tool is the teacher's monitoring book or logbook. The idea for this tool came from a teacher from New Zealand. Each teacher makes her or his own book for keeping track of each student's progress. This book is usually a three-ring binder in which a section is allotted to each child. The child's name is written on a tab for easy reference. Each child's section contains a pocket folder, several sheets of lined paper for writing notes and anecdotal information, and an assortment of other assessment tools and checklists. Some teachers include pages titled "Things I Know," "Things That I Am Working On," and "Books That I Have Read."

The various dated entries contain a wealth of information that the teacher uses throughout the year in conferencing with the children, in planning instruction, and in parent conferences. These entries attest to the observational skills of a teacher who has truly become a "kid-watcher"!

The monitoring notebook helps teachers address several of the stated functions of our assessment plan. Because we believe that language must be assessed in real situations, teachers use their monitoring notebooks throughout the day to record students' use of appropriate strategies and skills during independent work periods and group discussions. This tool also helps us make instructional decisions based on the information we collect.

When teachers like Penny Strube listen as students discuss what they have read or confer with a student about a piece of writing or a classroom project, they often find it helpful to turn to that student's section of the monitoring notebook and jot down specific examples of her or his skills. These informal notes are usually referred to as "anecdotal records." Let's look at what Penny Strube recorded in her monitoring notebook as she listened to several of her fourth-grade students discuss the story of Helen Keller (see figure 6.8). As you read Penny's notes, notice how she translates what the students say into the specific skills or strategies that they are applying. For example, on 1-10-92 Penny recorded three specific points from her observation of Jennifer. In her monitoring notebook Penny wrote Jennifer's name, the date, and several excerpts from Jennifer's discussion of the Helen Keller story: "Helen can't see, hear or talk. Because she was disabled. Fever was the cause, the effect was she couldn't see, hear, or talk. Predict she will be able to communicate." As we study Penny's original notes, we see that she recorded "MI" in a circle above the first notation "Helen can't see, hear or talk." This is Penny's abbreviation for "main idea," and she uses it here to note Jennifer's ability to detect the main idea of a paragraph. Over the next notation Penny wrote "cause & effect." Finally, she wrote "predict" over the last notation.

When she first began to use anecdotal recordkeeping as a form of assessment, Penny would simply jot down a student's actions and/or words. Later she analyzed her notes, looking for examples of a student's use of a particular strategy or skill. With practice, Penny has been able to consolidate this process. Often she can analyze skills and strategies, such as Jennifer's detection of main idea and cause and effect, while she is observing.

These notes, or anecdotal records, are an invaluable source of assessment information. They provide an accurate record not only of Jennifer's ability to apply three important skills but also of the context in which Jennifer applied these skills. Penny can quickly scan several weeks and even months of notations in order to assess whether Jennifer's application of these skills was a one-time event or if she has shown a steady

Figure 6.8

Melanie (1-8-92)   [P.O.V.]
Hate to be Helen because people
were afraid of her. She was wild [Summary]
and broke their toys.

(4)

Jennifer (1-8-92) [Setting] [Char.] [A.P.] the author's
Story takes [Mood] [P.O.]
purpose. Good book.
I wouldn't like [Relate] [Pers.] blind + deaf.
Hel[ler] [Char. Analysis] know bad from
good.

(5⁺)

Melanie (1-10-92)
Helen was excited when Annie [Contrasts]
came. Another [Compares] book sad. she dropped
it in a well. This book was diff.
[Summary]. She is [Recognizes] now beginning
to understand func.
[Draws Concl.]

(5)

Jennifer (1-10-92)
[M.I.] [Cause + Effect]
M.I. Helen can't see, hear or talk.
Because she was disabled. Fever
was the cause. Effect was
she couldn't see, hear, or talk.
[Predict] she will be able to
communicate.

(5⁺)

Melanie (1-15-92)   [Metaphore]
Helen was a bookworm. Someone
that always has a book in their [Draws Compl.]
hand. Her behavior is better.
(was absent 3 days)

(4)

Jennifer (1-15-92)   [Draws Concl.]
Her behavior has changed since
she can communicate. Helen learned [Summary]
enough words to understand. A.P. [A.P.]
is funny. [Cause + Effect] - Annie
learned. [Char. Analysis] 2 char.

(5⁺)

Melanie (1-17-92)   [Draws Conc.] A.P.
[Setting] college. [Cause + Effect]
Blind can do what we do. Helen
actually proved that. [Cause + Effect]
[Char. Analysis] - more adult, nice + kind.
Father's death didn't affect her work.
If Annie hadn't come she would have
been.

(5)

Jennifer (1-17-92)
[Setting] M.I. [M.I.]
met famous people - learned [Summarizing]
[Predict]
Favorite - Predict she will be
famous.

(5)

Melanie (1-22-92)
Nick name Deredevil Helen
Invited to White House since she was [Summary]
little. [Summary] Anne Sullivan (Macy)
wrote poem.

(4)

Jennifer (1-22-92)   [Sequence of events]
World War I - sequence of events.
[Draws Concl.]
Jamie was friend. Poem.
Speeches - blind + deaf people learn
I would [love] to be Helen because
of how much she did.

(4)

growth in her ability to apply these skills and strategies to a variety of materials, in a variety of contexts, and for a variety of purposes.

Children become very familiar with the monitoring book and feel free to point out entries that need to be made. Many times a child will ask the teacher or another adult in the room to make an entry in the book, saying something like "I'm the second green tab."

Some teachers find it cumbersome to carry around a three-ring binder, so they record their observations in various ways and then transfer this information to the monitoring notebook. Post-it notes, self-adhesive labels, blank paper marked off in squares or grids, and lined notebook paper have been used by teachers we know to record observational information. Whatever the method preferred by the teacher, the name of student and the date should be noted, and the notes should then be placed in chronological order.

It is important to stress that the monitoring notebook helps us keep track of what the children are and are not doing. An important device in the monitoring notebook is the list of skills and concepts that are generally addressed each year (figures 6.9 and 6.10). Because we do not use textbooks as curriculum guides, it is important that we have a way of keeping track of each student's progress in acquiring language and literacy skills. When teachers are consciously aware of the skills that the children should be able to apply, they are better able to help them achieve those skills through various demonstrations and projects.

Unlike traditional classrooms where teachers present skills in the order that they appear in a commercial text, teachers in whole language classrooms use their monitoring notebooks to help them decide when the students are ready to learn particular skills. For example, story theme can be particularly troublesome for many children, because it requires deep comprehension of the story. It is, nonetheless, an important goal in reading comprehension. A teacher who notes an absence of notations next to this particular item or skill in the monitoring notebook is in a better position to decide whether to give a lesson on the skill. For example, let's say a teacher becomes aware that some of the children never talk about the theme of a story or book. The teacher may decide to choose a book that has strong themes and to model various ways a reader might figure out the theme. She may then ask students to record in their literature logs the book's theme next to its title.

Penny Strube may give one of her fourth-grade literature groups a minilesson on figuring out an author's purpose for writing a story. In her minilesson, Penny tells the children that she would like them to use this skill whenever appropriate. In subsequent discussions Penny writes in her

Figure 6.9

OBSERVED SKILLS

Story Elements: Settings: / / / / / / /

Characters: / / / / / / /

Sequence: / / / / / / /

Narrator: / / / / / / /

Mood: / / / / / / /

Author's Purpose: / / / / / / /

Cause and Effect: / / / / / / /

Compares Characters: / / / / / / /

Contrasts Characters: / / / / / / /

Main Idea: / / / / / / /

Summarizes: / / / / / / /

Predicts Outcome: / / / / / / /

Draws Conclusions: / / / / / / /

Makes Generalizations: / / / / / / /

Identifies Problems: / / / / / / /

Solutions: / / / / / / /

Exaggerations: / / / / / / /

Similes: / / / / / / /

Metaphors: / / / / / / /

Relates Personally: / / / / / / /

Personal Point of View: / / / / / / / /

_____ / / / / / / / /

_____ / / / / / / / /

_____ / / / / / / / /

_____ / / / / / / / /

_____ / / / / / / / /

Penny Strube 4th

Figure 6.10

WRITING ASSESSMENT

MECHANICS:		Date	-,+	Date
Capitalization:	Beginning Sentences	( )	( )	( )
	Proper Nouns	( )	( )	( )
	Titles	( )	( )	( )
Punctuation:	Period	( )	( )	( )
	Question Mark	( )	( )	( )
	Exclamation	( )	( )	( )
	Semicolon	( )	( )	( )
	Colon	( )	( )	( )
Commas:	In a series	( )	( )	( )
	Direct Address	( )	( )	( )
	Yes and No	( )	( )	( )
	Dates	( )	( )	( )
	Explaining Phrase	( )	( )	( )
	Between City and State	( )	( )	( )
	After Greeting and Closing of a Letter	( )	( )	( )
	Between Clauses of Compound Sentences	( )	( )	( )
Quotation Marks:	Indent	( )	( )	( )
	Commas	( )	( )	( )
	End Punctuation	( )	( )	( )

PARTS OF SPEECH:

Nouns: Plurals
         Possessive: Singular ( ) ( ) ( ) Plural ( ) ( ) ( )

Pronouns:Personal (Used as subjects: I, you, he, she, it, we, they) ( ) ( ) ( )

         Possessive (mine, yours, his, her, its, theirs, ours) ( ) ( ) ( )

         Compound Personal
         (myself, yourself, himself, herself, itself, ourselves, themselves) ( ) ( ) ( )

Verbs:Linking (be, am, is, are, was, were, been) ( ) ( ) ( )

     Tense: Present ( ) Past ( ) Future( )

     Subject and Verb Agreement ( ) ( ) ( )

     Usage ( ) ( ) ( )

Adjectives: Positive ( ) ( ) Comparative (er) ( ) ( ) Superlative (est)( ) ( )

Adverb: Modifies a Verb ( ) ( ) ( )

       Modifies an Adjective ( ) ( ) ( )

Contractions ( ) ( ) ( )

Homophones: ( ) ( ) ( )

Figure 6.10 (Continued)

SENTENCE STRUCTURE:	Date		-,+		Date	
Run-on Sentences	(	)	(	)	(	)
Simple Sentences	(	)	(	)	(	)
Expanded Sentences with Details/Descriptors	(	)	(	)	(	)
Compound Sentences with Connectors (and, or, but)	(	)	(	)	(	)
Variety of Sentence Length, Style, Pattern	(	)	(	)	(	)
Uses Similes/Metaphors	(	)	(	)	(	)
Subject and Verb Agreement	(	)	(	)	(	)

WRITTEN EXPRESSION:						
Relates Content to Title	(	)	(	)	(	)
Uses Good Leads to Hook the Reader	(	)	(	)	(	)
Develops Plot	(	)	(	)	(	)
Develops Characters	(	)	(	)	(	)
Writing Contains:						
Focus	(	)	(	)	(	)
Beginning	(	)	(	)	(	)
Middle	(	)	(	)	(	)
Ending	(	)	(	)	(	)
Writes in: First Person (speaking)	(	)	(	)	(	)
Second Person (spoken to)	(	)	(	)	(	)
Third Person (spoken about)	(	)	(	)	(	)

TYPE OF WRITING:

Adventure (	)	Current Events (	)
Fantasies (	)	Folk Tales (	)
Fables (	)	Fiction (	)
History (	)	Hobbies (	)
Holidays (	)	Myths (	)
Nonfiction (	)	Novels (	)
Plays (	)	Poetry (	)
Personal Narratives (	)	Reports (	)
Science Fiction (	)	Sports (	)
Speeches (	)	Biography (	)

PENMANSHIP:						
Manuscript:	(	)	(	)	(	)
Cursive:	(	)	(	)	(	)
Spacing:	(	)	(	)	(	)
Uses Margins	(	)	(	)	(	)

Penny Strube
Monitoring Book

monitoring notebook examples of the students' use of the skill. When she is sure that a student has mastered the skill, she notes this in her book.

STUDENT PORTFOLIOS

Besides the monitoring notebook, the teacher keeps portfolios containing samples of the students' written work. The teachers at Oakwood make portfolios from brown expandable files with string closures. When a child enters our school for the first time, the teacher sets up a portfolio. In these large expandable envelopes are the artifacts of our assessment plan—the *products* that serve as testimony to the processes children have learned to apply.

Each child participates in developing his or her portfolio, and the portfolios at Oakwood are as varied and wonderful as the children themselves. A portfolio may contain, for example, poems, reports, photographs of projects, stories, videotapes, audiotapes, descriptions, and any number of other items, all chosen to depict the child's years of growth and development as a learner at Oakwood School.

Together, the child and the teacher decide which samples to include in the portfolio. While the portfolio usually contains examples of the student's best work, it may also hold reports that begin at the planning stage and continue through notetaking and final draft. Since the portfolio travels with the child from grade to grade, it serves as a wonderful exhibit of that child's growth and development throughout the elementary years.

While portfolios have worked well for us, there are other ways of accomplishing the same goal. Some schools set up Memory Books or scrapbooks that contain many of the same artifacts that we include in our brown expandable file folders. These scrapbooks may or may not be passed on from grade to grade, depending on the school. Sometimes the teachers and children work together to choose one or two samples that they feel best illustrate the child's achievement during that particular year. These samples are then stored in a cumulative folder that is forwarded to the teacher of each subsequent grade.

The portfolios are also used as a means of self-assessment. For example, Missy, a fourth-grader at Oakwood who has a portfolio containing four years of her best work, commented that she can't keep from smiling when she sees her early work. "I like what I wrote about," she says. "And for one so young, I think it is good. It was a lot easier to pick something to write about then. It is harder now. I am much pickier."

WRITING FOLDERS

Besides the portfolio, we have found it useful to have individual writing folders that contain each child's "works in progress." That is, all the pieces on which the child is currently working are kept in a special pocket folder. If we were to examine one of these writing folders we would typically find lists of topics that the child is interested in writing about, perhaps a list of writing skills that the child is working on, and maybe a list of commonly misspelled words. In addition, there would very likely be planning notes, webs, outlines, rough drafts, revising and editing suggestions, and so on, depending on how far along in the writing process the piece is. We might also find the beginnings of pieces that the child decided, for one reason or another, to temporarily abandon. It is through these unfinished pieces that the child learns that some initial ideas are best left for another time, perhaps after he or she has gathered more information. The children should be encouraged to save these pieces in case they want to come back to them later on in the year.

These writing folders yield important formative assessment information and are a valid means of documenting students' writing skills. They are also a rich source of information to use in parent conferencing, as teachers strive to show parents concrete evidence of "where their child is" with respect to language and literacy learning.

Finally, as we stated earlier, assessment informs instruction in a whole language classroom. As a teacher browses through a child's writing folder, she or he is in an excellent position to analyze both what the child can and cannot yet do in writing. The contents of the writing folder are a wonderful testimony to the writing process and enable an ongoing assessment of each child's progress in writing. At a glance the teacher can assess whether Mark needs help with interviewing skills or with making bibliography cards. She or he can quickly skim the folder to check on topic sentences and paragraph construction, noting whether the child needs further instruction in these areas. Perhaps the teacher is wondering how many children will need formal instruction in using the serial comma or quotation marks. By perusing the writing folders, she or he will be able to note which children have mastered these skills, which are having difficulty with them, and which have not attempted to use them. This information would be recorded in the monitoring notebook (see figure 6.11).

Again, this method contrasts with what we normally see in a traditional classroom, where the teacher gives lessons in the serial comma and quotation marks to the entire class, regardless of whether or not the children already know these skills or have a real need to know them at this particular time.

Figure 6.11

EVALUATION FORM FOR WRITING

Student Name _____

	Date ____			Date ____			Date ____		
	C	D	NE	C	D	NE	C	D	NE
WRITING QUALITY									
Self-selected topics									
Uses expansive vocabulary									
Uses complex sentences									
Experiments with different styles									
Uses revision strategies									
WRITING MECHANICS									
Handwriting									
Uses periods									
Uses quotation marks									
Uses exclamation points									
Uses question marks									
Uses capitalization									
Grammar usage									
Ratio and % invented spelling									
Ratio and % conventional spelling									

C = controls this
D = developing this
NE = no evidence of this

Comments and examples _____

_____

_____

_____

_____

_____

_____

EVALUATION SHEETS

In light of our belief about the integration of assessment and instruction, we place enormous value on teacher observation, anecdotal recordkeeping, portfolios of a student's work, student writing folders, and the monitoring notebook. The *evaluation sheet* is another teacher-developed tool that is used to evaluate the student's writing in authentic situations. It is also a good example of the many ways assessment informs instruction in a whole language classroom.

The evaluation sheet takes many different forms, depending on both the individual teacher and the different needs of the learners. The teacher usually issues the sheet to the child at the beginning of a project that requires writing, although some teachers attach the evaluation sheet to a child's rough draft. Simply stated, the evaluation sheet lists the elements that the child's final project should show. The sheet can, therefore, be personalized for each child in the class. For example, a first-grade teacher may include on the list "keep spaces between the words" or "the story must have a beginning, a middle, and an end." Similarly, a sixth-grader's sheet might say, "This report must include a bibliography and a table of contents." A sheet might include words that the child has recently misspelled as well as particular conventions, such as the serial comma or quotation marks, that the child needs to apply in this particular piece of writing.

Most of the evaluation sheets include a rating scale that the teacher uses to assign a numerical figure or percentage to each child's work. For example, Carol Brandt assigns a possible maximum score to each item or skill listed on her evaluation form (see figure 6.12). She uses the scale to evaluate the child's final product and then simply totals the scores.

The evaluation sheet might also contain more subjective criteria related to the student's project. Such is the case with the project evaluation sheet that Beth Taylor developed to use with fifth-grade students during one of their literature studies (see figure 6.13). The students are rated on a scale from 1 (poor) to 5 (excellent) on criteria ranging from "Report has proper punctuation and capitalization" to "Student used time wisely." In addition, Beth includes a place to record a daily numerical rating for discussion/ participation, literature log, oral reading, and comprehension. The oral reading section is subdivided into five areas, with each area to receive a maximum of two points for a total of ten points. The five areas are: reads for meaning, uses more than one strategy for solving unknown words, self-corrects, reads with expression, and reads for an audience. Similarly, the comprehension section includes four criteria that can receive up to five

Figure 6.12

WRITING EVALUATION FORM

Name _____ Date _____

Kind of Writing _____

Fill in the skills you wish to evaluate. Fill in a range of scores for a rating scale. Rate each skill on the rating scale and total the scores.

Skills checked	Rating Scale	
		MAXIMUM SCORE
Title _____	_____	3
Story/Sentence Clarity _____	_____	5
Paragraphs _____	_____	5
Punctuation - endmarks _____	_____	5
_____ quotation marks ____	_____	5
_____ commas _____	_____	5
Capitalization - Beginning of sentence	_____	5
_____ Proper nouns ____	_____	5
Apostrophes - Possessives _____	_____	5
_____ Contractions _____	_____	5

Comments:

Number of Words: _____

Handwriting: _____

Spelling: _____

Total _____ ____

Not all skills are applicable on all writings.

Carol Brandt - Grade 3

Figure 6.13

LITERATURE GROUP EVALUATION FORM

STUDENT'S NAME _____ DATE _____

LITERATURE SET _____

PROJECT _____

PROJECT EVALUATION:

     5 - Excellent 4 - Above Average 3 - Average 2 - Below Average 1 - Poor

1. _____ Report had title.
2. _____ Report had illustrations.
3. _____ Report was told in student's language.
4. _____ Report was creative and related to the book.
5. _____ Report has proper punctuation and capitalization.
6. _____ Report has proper spelling.
7. _____ Student used time wisely.
8. _____ Final project was edited and neat.

                                     Total points_____40 points possible

Discussion/Participation
1 - 5 Points per day
_____ Monday
_____ Tuesday
_____ Wednesday
Total points_____
15 points possible

Literature Log
1 - 5 Points per day
_____ Monday
_____ Tuesday
_____ Wednesday
Total points_____
15 points possible

Oral Reading
1 - 2 points possible
_____ Reads for meaning.
_____ Uses more than one
       strategy for solving
       unknown words.
_____ Reader self-corrects.
_____ Reads with expression.
_____ Reads for an audience.
Total points _____
10 Points possible

Comprehension
1 - 5 points possible
_____ Setting/Character

_____ Problem
_____ Solution
_____ Sequence of events

Total points _____
20 Points possible

                                   Beth Taylor
                                   Grade 5

points each for a total of twenty points. The criteria are: setting/character, problem, solution, and sequence of events.

As part of their involvement in a thematic study of animals, each student in Carol Brandt's third-grade classroom at Oakwood used her or his growing knowledge of the writing process to research and develop a report about one animal. The students began by creating webs containing facts they already knew about their chosen animals. Before students began to read and take notes, they evaluated their webs and conferenced with Carol, who shared her evaluation with each student. As the students progressed through the writing process, they self-evaluated and conferenced *before* going on to the next stage. Carol used evaluation sheets for each stage of the process. Figure 6.14 shows the sheet she used to evaluate the students' abilities to participate effectively in the final stage of the writing process—sharing their work with others.

Figure 6.14

ANIMAL REPORTS

Student's Name _____
Date _____
Subject _____

Report Evaluation
    5 Always
    4 Usually
    3 Sometimes
    2 Seldom
    1 Never

_____ Report was introduced with a title.
_____ Report was given in student's own language.
_____ Student spoke loudly.
_____ Student spoke clearly.
_____ Student gave report without looking at notes.
_____ Student had good knowledge of subject.
_____ Student included a visual aid with report.
_____ Student could answer questions presented by the audience.
_____ Student took the oral report seriously.

_____ Total
_____ Percent

STANDARDIZED TESTING

Every school tries to score well on standardized tests, and Oakwood is no exception. Many times standardized tests are used to compare schools within a state or district. In recent years, the importance assigned to standardized test scores has increased tremendously . According to Nolan, Haladyna, and Haas (1992), "Some form of standardized achievement testing is mandatory in forty-two of the fifty states" (p. 9). Further, according to the results of the 1989 Gallup poll, 77 percent of the respondents supported the use of standardized achievement tests to measure the academic achievement of students. So, not to address what our school does with respect to standardized testing would be to avoid an issue that continues to pose dilemmas.

Like so many other whole language schools, Oakwood often undergoes more scrutiny than traditional schools. This presents a challenge for most whole language teachers. Because they are designing their own curriculum, whole language teachers are very aware of the knowledge, skills, and attitudes that are appropriate at each stage of development. And because their instruction is so individualized, whole language teachers are more aware of each student's abilities and needs than traditional teachers, who rely on an end-of-level basal test to reveal individual children's strengths and weaknesses. As we emphasized in an earlier section, instruction and assessment are intertwined in whole language classrooms; the teachers do not wait for a test to tell them that the children need instruction in any area. Rather, their assessment strategies enable them to deal with a specific skill as soon as a child needs it. This is a much more efficient way to teach than the old "test/reteach/test" model, which assumes that at least a certain percentage of youngsters need "reteaching."

Standardized tests can be intimidating to classroom teachers. However, whole language teachers have an edge, so to speak, because they already know their students so well. Unlike traditional teachers who often have not accumulated artifacts that document each student's progress, the whole language teacher has a wealth of information with which to document, explain, and if necessary justify children's development. By their very nature, the majority of standardized tests deal with isolated skills and bits of information on the recall level. Typically, in grades three and above the children in whole language classrooms are able to adapt to the format of the standardized test, even though they have spent very little, if any, classroom time on similarly formatted tasks. Unfortunately, at the lower grade levels the children's scores are generally much more affected by the format of the tests. Compared with children who complete workbook and skill sheets daily, the children in whole language classrooms tend to score lower. While this can be unsettling, our teachers have had to take precautions against devoting precious classroom time to teaching students to use a format that does not contribute to their learning. Just before giving the tests, the teachers do spend a small amount of time teaching "test literacy." In most classrooms this involves modeling how to choose "the best answer" to a question and giving the children practice exercises.

Another finding about standardized test scores is that students in whole language classrooms tend to score higher on measures of comprehension and lower on measures of isolated decoding or word analysis skills. This finding is certainly not surprising, given the nature of a whole language program. At Oakwood, reading comprehension scores and math problem-solving scores are now either higher than or equal to the scores in language mechanics or math computation. Also, tests at Oakwood show a high retention rate in social studies and science, which we attribute to our use of thematic units of study.

The assessment tools described earlier in this section provide much more valid information about individual pupil progress than standardized test scores. We do, however, see some value in having both contextualized and decontextualized assessment measures. Contextualized assessment measures are those used within the ongoing classroom curriculum. At Oakwood these include various checklists and teacher-made tests as well as the Miscue Analysis Inventory discussed earlier. Decontextualized assessment measures are used independently of the ongoing classroom curriculum. The Missouri Mastery Test and various norm and criterion-referenced tests are in this category. At Oakwood results of standardized tests are used to help us align the curriculum rather than to assess a student's progress. For this information we rely on newer and more effective assessment measures.

PERFORMANCE TESTING

The current controversy surrounding standardized tests and the real erosion of confidence in these tests have led to the development of performance-based measures for evaluating students' progress. During the 1992 school year, Oakwood teachers developed and piloted the Performance Reading and Writing Evaluation. This tool was inspired by a presentation that Roger Farr of the University of Indiana made at the 1992 Missouri State Reading Council convention. In his speech Farr described an experiment that he had conducted with young children. The children were asked to read a selection on carnivorous plants. Then they were asked to write a piece that included remarks that a mother bug would make to her children. By sharing a sample of the children's writing, Farr was able to effectively demonstrate an alternative to standardized tests.

The Oakwood version of this assessment tool includes an expository selection that students at each grade read independently. They then use the knowledge gained by reading the selection to develop a piece of writing. For example, the second-grade children were given an article about owls to read, after which they wrote about what a mother mouse would say to her children about owls. The fourth-grade students read a piece about birds' ability to fly. For their writing task they assumed the role of a mother bird and wrote advice for her baby birds (see figure 6.15).

The students were allowed a number of days to complete the task. They could revise and edit as much as they wanted; however, they had to work independently. All the children's writings were scored according to a numerical rating scale that was adopted for use by the Department of Education in Missouri (see figure 6.16). Next, the percentages, by grade level, of students scoring in each category were determined. The insights gained from this assessment tool were useful in a number of areas. First of all, comparing each child's writing to a standard, such as to the numerical rating scale, helped teachers decide what areas to stress during regular class time. Teachers were also able to identify children who were having difficulty in certain areas of reading and in using the information in their writing. Finally, this task has helped us document how many of our children can read and respond in writing to grade-appropriate information. Calculating the percentages of students above, at, and below average helps us make curricular decisions and also provides us with base-line data that we can use as we work with children to increase their reading and writing abilities.

Saying Yes to Accountability!

In a whole language school such as Oakwood, assessment information is used not only to inform teachers, children, and parents about educational achievement and progress but also to convince school board members, representatives of state boards and accreditation agencies, members of the community, and other educators of the effectiveness of a whole language approach to learning. We are just beginning to realize how powerful these assessment strategies are. However, assessment is usually the last component addressed in the development of a new program. It bears repeating that

Figure 6.15

You are a parent bird. You have young birds that are ready to learn to fly and leave the nest. What would you tell them about flying, their ancestors, and the world that awaits them?

"Now my little birdlings come stand, in a row."
"There is one thing important that all you should know." "We are a bird of prey. We have to hunt to get a meal every day." "We can eat any kind of meat like a hare, bear. We're the real Masters of air." "We can fly non-stop from bottom to top." said, Mother Eagle. You must jump up and flap, then when you get the hang of flying, you look down and when you see and smell food, swop down" and get it. Know another thing I need to exsplain, is how fast you should go. You can reach 150 miles and (240 Km) per hour. In the winter of course to keep warm we move different places and still as a bird of pray we can be killed any old day. The Human of course are the worest, they kill us for fun so we can lay in the sun. Dead!!!

Figure 6.16

OAKWOOD PERFORMANCE
READING AND WRITING ASSESSMENT

5

The paper contains clear controlling idea that specifically addresses the article, revealing some complexity and/or freshness of thought. It has a beginning, middle, and end. It makes a distinction between main and subordinate ideas. It contains language that is precise and perhaps vivid. The sentences vary in structure, with few errors in grammar and mechanics.

4

The paper contains a competent controlling idea with a sense of direction, and it adequately addresses the article. It has evidence of a beginning, middle, and end. It uses some specific details, but it may rely more on general statements to support main and subordinate ideas. The paper may contain language that is inconsistent and uneven. The paper contains clear sentences that may lack variety in structure and may have errors in grammar and mechanics.

3

The paper, although addressing the article, has a controlling idea that is not adequately developed. It may have some evidence of a beginning, middle, and end, but it may lack cohesion and at times seem disjointed. It relies on generalities and few specific details. It contains sentences that are fairly clear, but errors in grammar, language, and mechanics may be distracting.

2

The paper contains one or more ideas that address the article, but none that controls development. Although lacking cohesion, the paper may have some evidence of a beginning, middle, and end or may be a simple listing of ideas. It may contain sentences that are unclear as well as repeated errors in grammar, language, mechanics, or sentence structure.

1

The paper lacks a controlling idea and only momentarily address the article. It may lack a sense of organization and/or development. It contains may sentences that are confusing as well as frequent and repeated errors in grammar, language, mechanics, and structure.

whole language assessment helps us better understand ourselves and our children. It is the hub of our curriculum.

When teachers have a clear picture of what assessment in a whole language classroom is really all about, they begin to use it differently. Their conferences with parents no longer center around grades. They do not compare children with other children and discourage parents from doing so. They talk with each other about what children are *doing* rather than what *grades* children are making. They begin to trust more in their own professional judgment and in the children's ability to evaluate their own strengths and areas of need. Teachers constantly work to improve their "kidwatching" techniques, and they share new recordkeeping devices and skills with one another. Finally, teachers report that they *know their children* better than they ever did before. As a result, staffings held for children who are being considered for special programs are more revealing and substantive, and there is a much closer match between instruction and the needs and abilities of each child.

At Oakwood, assessment does not "drive" instruction, as is the case in many schools. Rather, assessment and instruction go hand in hand as teachers bring the children and the curriculum together.

All schools, traditional and whole language, need to begin to assess their thinking about assessment. We need to think of assessment, not in terms of grading, but rather as a way of explaining what children can do and need to be able to do next. When this is accomplished, our schools will be well on the way to becoming *performance-based* rather than *grade-driven*. As John Holt says, perhaps then "children will not have to be bribed and bullied to acquire the skills of reading and writing, they will want them for what they can do with them" (1976).

A POSTSCRIPT FROM ELIZABETH . . .

So, what did I share with the superintendent from St. Louis? He saw a first-grade monitoring book full of notes and observations made by the teacher, a number of children's portfolios, and a child's writing folder containing several drafts of the child's work with evaluation sheets clipped to each. By examining each of these "artifacts," he was able to construct a clear picture of the child's progress, and in so doing, was also able to verify the accountability of the classroom teacher.

REFERENCES:

– **Anderson, R. C., Hiebert, E. H., Scott, J. A., & Wilkinson, L. A. G.** (1985). *Becoming a nation of readers: The report of the commission on reading*. Washington,DC: National Institute of Education.

– **Brown, R.** (1989). Testing and thoughtfulness. *Educational Leadership, 46,* 31–34.

– **Cannell, J. J.** (1988). Nationally normed elementary achievement testing in America's public schools: How all 50 states are above the national average. *Educational Measurement: Issues and Practice, 7,* 5–9.

– **Gallup, A. M.** (1989). The 21st annual Gallup poll of public's attitude toward the public schools. *Phi Delta Kappan, 71,* 39–54.

– **Goodman, K.** (1969). Analysis of oral reading miscues: Applied psycholinguistics. *Reading Research Quarterly, 5,* 9–30.

– **Goodman, Y.** (1978). Kidwatching: An alternative to testing. *The National Elementary Principal, 57,* 41–55.

– **Goodman, Y. M., & Burke, C. L.** (1972). *The reading miscue inventory*. New York: Macmillan.

– **Graves, D., & Hansen, J.** (1987). The Author's Chair. *Language Arts, 60,* 176–183.

– **Hansen, J.** (1987). *When writers read*. Portsmouth, NH: Heinemann.

– **Hiebert, E. H., & Calfee, R. C.** (1992). Assessing literacy: From standardized tests to portfolios and performances. In *What research has to say about reading instruction* (2nd ed., pp. 70–100). Newark, DE: International Reading Association.

– **Holt, J.** (1976). *How children fail*. New York: Dell Publishing Company.

– **Johnston, P. H., Weiss, P. B., & Afflerbach, P.** (1989). *Teachers' evaluation of teaching and learning in literacy and literature*. Albany, NY: Center for the Learning and Teaching of Literature.

– **Kamii, C., & Kamii, M.** (Eds.) 1990. *Achievement testing in the early grades: The games grown-ups play*. Washington, DC: National Association for the Education of Young Children.

– **Lamme, L. L., & Hysmith, C.** (1991). One school's adventure into portfolio assessment. *Language Arts, 60,* 629–640.

– **Nolan, S. B., Haladyna, T. M., & Haas, N. S.** (1992). Uses and abuses of achievement test scores. *Educational Measurement: Issues and Practice, 11(2),* 9–15.

– **Perrone, V.** (1991). On standardized testing. *Childhood Education,* 132–142. Wheaton, MD: Association for Childhood Education International.

– **Shepard, L.** (1988, April). Should instruction be measurement-driven? Paper presented at the annual meeting of the American Educational Research Association, New Orleans, LA.

– **Tierney, R. J., & Pearson, P. D.** (1984). Toward a composing model of reading. In J. M. Jenson (Ed.), *Composing and comprehending* (pp. 33–46). Urbana, IL: National Conference on Research in English.

– **Weaver, C.** (1992). A whole language belief system and its implications for teacher and institutional change. In Weaver, C., & Henke, L. (Eds.), *Supporting whole language* (pp. 3–23). Portsmouth, NH: Heinemann.

CHAPTER SEVEN

Staying Whole: The Importance of Professional Growth and Development

---

A NOTE FROM ELIZABETH . . .

It would be very difficult to call any school a whole language school without realizing that being a whole language school means that there exists a constant search for ways to make what goes on in classrooms better for both children and teachers. This valuing of the process of self-examination results in a school whose staff is constantly changing and growing. Because whole language teachers are so dedicated to meeting the needs of all children, to remain static would violate their beliefs. This should also be true for the school administrator.

Every year the needs of each staff member are somewhat different. And every year the skills and abilities of each staff member continue to change and grow. Obviously, professional growth plans for a first-year teacher differ from those of returning staff members; therefore, for an administrator to attempt to set down a formula for "taking care of" the professional growth and development of all teachers would violate what we know about how learning best occurs.

In the teaching profession we tout the phrase "a teacher is a life-long learner." Not surprisingly, teacher education candidates seldom understand the true weight of this statement. When we confer on an individual the title of teacher, we are also placing on her or him the tremendous responsibility of keeping current in the field of education. This is not a responsibility that should be taken lightly. As the old joke goes, "That teacher didn't really teach twenty-five years . . . she just taught one year twenty-five times!" While we might laugh at the absurdity of this statement, deep down we fear that, for certain teachers, this "joke" might be a reality. School administrators play a very important role in fostering the continued professional growth and development of classroom teachers.

A NOTE FROM KATHY . . .

University graduate courses have always been a primary vehicle for continuing professional growth for classroom teachers. However, the degree of personal change that results from graduate courses is variable, to say the least. As we discussed in chapter three, a key component of

*change efforts in teaching involves the active participation of teachers in
setting their own agendas for professional development. Although this
can be accomplished in a variety of ways, the goals and objectives of
both the courses and the teachers enrolled in the courses must be met. In
an effort to promote and support changes in both beliefs and teaching
practices, I generally ask teachers to examine their personal belief systems
and current teaching practices in light of the course content. An
important assignment as the course draws to a close involves
anticipating future action(s) based on the course experience. As a
professor, I feel most successful when the papers that result from this
assignment include a stated desire and/or need for continued
professional growth.*

*In her paper, Louise, a kindergarten teacher, writes, "I have by no
means exhausted all of the information available in the books and
articles. I imagine that I will be spending a great deal of this summer
reading and pre-planning my curriculum for next year," thus revealing
an intent to, through continued study and reflection, put into action
new strategies and ideas gained during the semester. Similarly, Pam
Campbell, a first-grade teacher, discussed how having to choose from
among the course materials a number of strategies to "try out" in her
classroom forced her to take some needed steps toward change, "I found
the study-application guide for each text reading to be the most useful
for me. This forced me to do the required readings as well as apply what
I read in my own classroom. It is one thing to read about what you
should be doing if you are an teacher. It is even better to be forced to DO
what you should to be an effective classroom teacher. I hope to stay
focused and continue what you have encouraged me to get started."
Statements such as these from Louise and Pam indicate a commitment to
continued professional growth and development. As a self-proclaimed
"change agent," I do not take these words lightly. . . .*

*The purpose of this chapter is to offer some suggestions for school
administrators who are striving to help teachers, in Pam's words, "stay
focused" and continue to grow and develop as professionals who adhere
to a whole language philosophy of learning. With this in mind, we
suggest in this chapter four general areas that need to be addressed in
order to maintain a whole language philosophy in a school. These areas
are: teacher evaluation, inservice education, professional reading, and
classroom research. In the pages that follow we present some general
information regarding these four areas and then share specific examples
based on our experiences at Oakwood.*

Schoolwide Planning for Ongoing Professional Development

In chapter three we discussed characteristics of effective staff development and the formation of a school or district plan for improvement. Such a plan could be used during many of the different phases or stages through which a school might evolve. For example, in chapter three we emphasized plans for developing a whole language program and then for implementing that program. Once the program is in place, however, the plans take on a new look as the emphasis shifts to maintenance. Like any plan, the maintenance plan must take into account the desires and needs of individuals on the teaching staff and of the group as a whole. And the plan must be tailored to fit each school and/or school district. This, of course, means that many individuals must be involved in setting goals and objectives for professional growth and development and in choosing activities that help accomplish individual as well as collective goals and objectives.

Because of his or her ongoing and careful observation of and participation in various classroom activities, the school administrator is in a unique position to offer suggestions for professional growth activities aimed at benefiting the overall school program. More than any other member of the educational team, the school administrator must be ever mindful of the responsibility for assuring the success of a program that adheres to the school's stated philosophy of learning. The school administrator uses a solid base of knowledge about whole language to illuminate each classroom observation.

A NOTE FROM ELIZABETH . . .

I remember a time when I was working with one child. The administrator came to the door to observe me, and on seeing me with the child said, "I'll come back when you are teaching." I know now as an administrator what I knew then as a teacher—that to observe a teacher working with one child is to witness some of the most efficient teaching one can possibly see . . . and it happens a lot in a whole language classroom!

Part of the administrator's role in creating a schoolwide plan for continued growth and development is to collect and analyze information from a variety of sources, such as classroom observations; informal interviews with teachers, students, parents, and community members; and evaluation of student progress. The administrator constantly analyzes this information in order to determine areas of both strengths and liabilities. The liabilities become targets for improvement. If the administrator notes that the activities students are engaged in are not constructive or are incompatible with the school's stated beliefs, he or she takes steps to rectify this situation. The administrator may want to arrange for inservice activities and professional readings on cooperative group learning, independent seatwork activities, learning centers, and so on as part of the schoolwide plan. Additionally, he or she may organize visits to classrooms in that and other schools.

A Note from Elizabeth . . .

I can remember how difficult it was for us when we first began to change the way we were assessing pupil progress. We were implementing whole language instruction—but we needed to make our assessment match our instruction. Included in our schoolwide plan were mini-workshops held in the library either before or after school. In our struggle to learn to apply holistic evaluation techniques we put examples of children's work on an overhead projector and practiced analyzing and recording assessment information. We taped children reading and speaking and discussed and analyzed what behaviors they were exhibiting. We were so accustomed to having children fill out worksheets for us to score and then record percentages earned that it was difficult for us to listen to a child's oral language in order to assess comprehension. I must remember those struggles as I work with the new teachers who come into our building.

Just as teachers work to build a feeling of community in their classrooms, the administrator must do likewise within the entire school building. The two most important elements in a school community are creating a democracy in which teachers have choices and providing opportunities for teachers to negotiate the rules. As in any democracy, these rules are based on an understanding that everyone will fulfill her or his individual and collective responsibilities; however, allowances exist for individual differences in meeting these responsibilities. For example, guided by statewide curriculum goals and budget issues, teachers at Oakwood have choices as to the themes they develop, the resources they purchase, the furniture they use, their plans for assessment, and their communications with parents. Additionally, since uninterrupted classroom time is highly valued at Oakwood, the teachers have the freedom to negotiate the scheduling of special classes such as physical education, music, art, Chapter I, learning disabilities, and speech and language. They hold informal discussions on how to manage hallway traffic, lunchroom conduct, and so forth, because these decisions are best made jointly by all involved. Likewise, parent involvement strategies work best when planned by the teachers rather than by just the administrator.

A Note from Elizabeth . . .

Each year at Oakwood, a schoolwide theme helps build a relationship between classes and serves as a valuable "community builder" for the whole school. "Caretakers of the Earth," the theme during 1991-92, set the tone for the entire year. The children were given keychain globes as they entered the school on the first day. T-shirts, projects, posters, and banners all espoused the importance of taking care of each other and of our planet. The theme for the following year, "Caretakers Celebrate Discoveries," came naturally as we celebrated the 500th anniversary of the voyage of Columbus. To prepare for this schoolwide theme, the teachers wrote to the children during the summer to ask them to begin to think of projects and activities that would help the class become aware of all the discoveries and discoverers shaping world history.

In addition to these schoolwide themes, we have a climate committee that functions informally every year. This climate committee began when the fourth- and fifth-grade teachers returned to school after attending a drug prevention inservice workshop. The ideas they implemented for establishing a positive climate in the classroom spread throughout the school. Now the climate committee plans parties and other functions that create a positive climate schoolwide.

The feeling of community is also strengthened by the monthly coffees held in the teachers' workroom. These before-school coffees are a time to share ideas, books, journal articles, and information from conferences as well as to plan programs and deal with problems. Earlier in our move toward a whole language philosophy we also had informal nightly meetings in the school library, which teachers could attend for additional support, ideas, or information.

Creating a schoolwide spirit of cooperation and congeniality is not something that happens accidentally; it is a planned effort. The administrator plays a critical role in establishing this feeling of community that serves to not only support but also sustain lasting changes.

Facilitating the Professional Growth of Individual Teachers

In addition to being a catalyst for the continued success of the overall school program, the school administrator plays a vital role in evaluating teachers. As we discussed earlier, one of the most important features in a whole language classroom is student self-evaluation. As we have found, the learner benefits greatly when evaluation criteria are: (1) made explicit for that learner and (2) used by each learner as a tool for self-assessment. Further, when teachers enlist the students' help in developing plans for improving their work, the students can better understand and carry out the necessary tasks. In a whole language school such as Oakwood, teacher evaluation adheres as closely as possible to the characteristics of a whole language philosophy that underlie the school's program. If we accept as part of our philosophy that teachers are guides to or facilitators of knowledge, skills, and attitudes, it seems logical that we apply this same philosophy to our understanding of the administrator's role in teacher evaluation. Similarly, if we believe that learning is both personal and social and that all educational settings should be learning communities, then *all* growth opportunities—those for teachers and administrators as well as for children—should reflect this belief. It is with these understandings and convictions in mind that the thoughtful administrator works with individual teachers to identify both the strengths and the liabilities in their classrooms. The knowledge the administrator gains from this interaction enables her or him to help teachers plan their professional growth.

Oakwood's Plan for Teacher Evaluation

While performance-based teacher evaluation is one tool for bringing about change, it is also a critical part of our plan for maintaining changes and for continued growth and development. As we discussed briefly in chapter three, we have implemented a system of performance-based teacher evaluation at Oakwood.

Missouri state law dictates that all probationary teachers receive a summative evaluation every year for five years, when they achieve tenure. After this time, they receive a summative evaluation every three years. Teachers receive formative evaluations every year except for the year in which a summative evaluation is given, when they receive two formative evaluations.

The *summative* evaluation (see figure 7.1) includes fifteen criteria, or job-related performance expectations. For each criterion, the administrator marks whether the teacher "meets expectations" or "does not meet expectations." The *formative* evaluation consists of an observation period, when the administrator writes a narrative describing what she or he sees and hears in each classroom. The administrator then transfers this information to a standardized formative form, which she or he shares with the teacher during a conference.

Because this procedure is mandated by law, administrators feel pressured to make the required number of observations. What is perhaps more important is that this process can be used not only to document teacher performance but also to instigate changes. For it to be an instrument of change, however, it is important that the teachers understand that the process is not a "dog-and-pony show." The teacher is not expected to "perform" while the administrator watches. In fact, the teacher may be observing the children while the administrator observes both teacher and children. Thus the criteria on the summative evaluation record will be valid and meaningful even when there is no direct teaching taking place.

A NOTE FROM ELIZABETH . . .
Paula Ingebretson's first-grade class was celebrating "one-hundred

Figure 7.1

HANNIBAL SCHOOL DISTRICT SUMMATIVE EVALUATION REPORT

Teacher: _____ School: _____

Performance Area: Instructional Process

The teacher:

A. Demonstrates evidence of lesson and unit planning and preparation.

____ Meets expectations   ____ Does not meet expectations

B. Demonstrates knowledge of curriculum and subject matter.

____ Meets expectations   ____ Does not meet expectations

C. Uses effective teaching techniques, strategies and skills during lesson.

____ Meets expectations   ____ Does not meet expectations

D. Uses instructional time effectively.

____ Meets expectations   ____ Does not meet expectations

E. Evaluates student progress effectively.

____ Meets expectations   ____ Does not meet expectations

F. Provides for individual differences.

____ Meets expectations   ____ Does not meet expectations

G. Demonstrates ability to motivate students.

____ Meets expectations   ____ Does not meet expectations

H. Establishes and maintains a classroom climate conducive to learning.

____ Meets expectations   ____ Does not meet expectations

I. Manages student behavior in a constructive manner.

____ Meets expectations   ____ Does not meet expectations

COMMENTS:

Performance Area: Interpersonal Relationships

The teacher:

A. Demonstrates positive interpersonal relationships with students.

____ Meets expectations   ____ Does not meet expectations

B. Demonstrates positive interpersonal relationships with educational staff.

____ Meets expectations   ____ Does not meet expectations

C. Demonstrates positive interpersonal relationships with parents and other members of the school community.

____ Meets expectations   ____ Does not meet expectations

COMMENTS:

Performance Area: Professional Responsibilities

The teacher:

A. Follows the policies, regulations and procedures of the school and district.

____ Meets expectations   ____ Does not meet expectations

B. Assumes responsibilities outside the classroom.

____ Meets expectations   ____ Does not meet expectations

C. Demonstrates a commitment to professional growth.

____ Meets expectations   ____ Does not meet expectations

COMMENTS:

Evaluator's Recommendation:

____ Reemployment recommended.   ____ Reemployment not recommended.

TEACHER'S COMMENTS:

EVALUATOR'S COMMENTS:

_____   _____

Teacher's Signature/Date   Evaluator's Signature/Date

(Signatures imply the content of this document has been discussed. Explanatory comments required for all ratings not meeting expected performance.)

day." The children had been counting days all year and were going to celebrate when they got to the one-hundredth day. They invited me to the party. The games at this party turned out to be learning centers that were placed all around the room. As I observed at one center, the children were giving each child at the center an equal number of hearts from a cup that contained 100 candy hearts. I watched as the leader donned a pair of plastic gloves and proceeded to distribute the hearts, one at a time. His leadership was quickly challenged when members of the group noted that this method was taking too much time. One child said, "Give us each two at a time," while other children suggested "Count them by fives." The leader responded by saying, "I need to read them before I give them to you," to which the children exclaimed, "We'll read them before we eat them!"

Had I been in Paula's room to evaluate her performance, I would have noted a number of teaching objectives that were being met through this one activity. The children were practicing counting to 100 as well as counting by twos and fives. They were also following directions, solving problems, negotiating with peers, showing initiative, and using sound-symbol relationships and context clues to help them read the directions for the task.

In a whole language classroom, the teacher's performance may not be as obvious as it is in a traditional classroom, where direct teaching takes place most of the time. However, when we evaluate what the children are doing we see concrete evidence of teacher performance that needs to be recognized and documented. When we see children taking responsibility for their own learning, demonstrating that they are becoming thinkers and problem solvers, we know a great deal about their classroom teacher. The learning centers in a whole language classroom speak volumes about the teacher's knowledge about how children learn and also about the amount of time the teacher devotes to planning and creating curriculum for and with the children. The role that indirect teaching plays in a whole language classroom is easy to document and is as important as the direct teaching that administrators have traditionally focused on.

Another part of Oakwood's performance-based system for evaluation is the Professional Growth Plan (see figure 7.2) that every teacher must complete. The criterion the teacher chooses may be general, such as "Uses instructional time effectively," or specific, such as "What teaching strategies work best with the children in my whole language classroom?" For example, Penny Strube asked the question "How do I get fourth-graders to do a better job of revising their writing?" To answer this question, and to fulfill her Professional Growth Plan, she read everything she could find about the writing process. Then she used this information to choose several strategies to implement. She took notes

Figure 7.2

HANNIBAL SCHOOL DISTRICT PROFESSIONAL GROWTH PLAN

❑ Enrichment
❑ Improvement

Teacher _____ School _____ Date _____

CRITERION:

State here a criterion, e.g., Uses instructional time effectively.

OBJECTIVE(S):

State the desired objective (outcome) to be accomplished. This will often be similar to a descriptor for that criterion.

PROCEDURES FOR ACHIEVING OBJECTIVE(S):

Provide specific statements which describe what the teacher is to do to achieve an objective and what the supervisor will do to assist. This is the process, the steps and the ingredients for change.

ASSESSMENT METHOD AND DATES:

How will we know when progress is made? How will we monitor that progress?
What are the short-term and long-term target dates?

COMMENTS:

COMMENTS:

Plan Developed   _____   _____
                        Teacher Signature/Date   Evaluator's Signature/Date

If Plan Revised (Date/Initials): _____

If Alternate Plan Developed (Date/Initials): _____

Plan Achieved   _____   _____
                        Teacher Signature/Date   Evaluator's Signature/Date

about what she tried, how each strategy worked, how the students responded, and so forth. She also collected samples of the children's writing. Over time, she began to observe remarkable improvement in the way her children revised their writing. She had achieved her Professional Growth Plan and in the process had effected a major curricular improvement.

Each teacher identifies curricular concerns in one or more of the following areas: learning, teaching, program strategies and/or activities, evaluation, parental involvement (Watson, Burke, & Harste, 1989). Although the administrator must ensure that the criteria each teacher chooses reflect a curricular concern (because ownership is a necessary ingredient for change), teachers rather than administrators need to make the final choice as to what particular criterion she will address. The administrator may discuss concerns and suggest what criterion to address and how to address it, but the teachers must be empowered to develop their own Professional Growth Plans.

A NOTE FROM ELIZABETH . . .

One criterion included in our evaluation is "Evaluates student progress effectively." At Oakwood, attention to this criterion served as a catalyst to effect instructional change. A discussion of the value of workbook pages and end-of-level basal tests ensued when the administrator asked a teacher to explain how assessment information was used to inform the teacher and the parents of the child's developmental level. Thus the performance evaluation was the starting point of the administrator's efforts to help a teacher, strategy by strategy, make learning more meaningful for her students.

A third strategy for teacher evaluation used at Oakwood involves keeping a portfolio for each teacher. These are kept in the principal's office and are considered confidential. As with the portfolios kept by the children in the school, anything that a teacher thinks is important can be included. For example, some teachers include copies of parent newsletters, curricular webs they have developed, proposals for conference presentations, or manuscripts they have submitted for publication. These insightful portfolios are a wonderful communication link between teacher and administrator and help develop teachers' self-evaluation skills as they seek to include articles that represent their very best work.

Professional Meetings and Inservice Workshops

Opportunities for professional growth and development of all teachers have reached new heights during the past few years. There are many opportunities for study. Virtually every professional educational organization holds conventions and conferences at least once a year, and most of these organizations have local, state, regional, and national affiliates that host their own separate activities. It is not unusual for local affiliates to have monthly or bimonthly meetings or staff development opportunities. These professional organizations are not alone in hosting professional growth opportunities. There are a number of private educational firms such as Good Apple of Carthage, Illinois, and the Learning Institute of Palo Alto, California, that offer various inservice workshops and the number of offerings multiplies each year. Participants in these conferences usually must pay a rather high fee for registration and materials. Transportation, meals, and lodging are extra.

Because of their many and varied choices, schools must decide carefully about which activities will help teachers accomplish individual goals and objectives and at the same time contribute to the overall school or district plan for improvement. Making these choices is not easy. Both teachers and administrators will want to know as much as possible about the organization or firm sponsoring the activity. It is important to find out about the speakers and their expertise and experience as well as about the level of background knowledge or experience of the average attendee. For example, attending a workshop titled "Whole Language" or even "Whole Language Evaluation" doesn't guarantee that the participant's particular needs or interests will be addressed. Chances are great that the workshop will be on a very basic, introductory level, unless otherwise specified in the promotional materials. While it helps to hear a message that reaffirms our beliefs and practices, most of us have had the disappointing experience of attending a session or institute where the speaker presented information with which we were already all too familiar.

It is sometimes more beneficial to seek out staff development activities by speaker rather than by topic. There are some speakers whose sessions we always attend, regardless of topic, because we know their work and that we will benefit from getting firsthand information. This is not to say that we have prior knowledge of all of those whose sessions we attend, for many whole language educators are now generously sharing their expertise with others. Among these are classroom teachers and administrators who daily face the challenge of putting their beliefs into practice. We have gained a great deal of knowledge and understanding and many practical, classroom-tested ideas from these professionals. But given the many choices in staff development offerings and the limited resources of most schools, teachers must choose carefully.

Teachers at Oakwood are encouraged to attend conferences. The school provides each teacher with registration fees and release time to attend one conference a year. Although lack of funds prevents the school from paying additional conference expenses, the teachers are often willing to pay their own hotel and travel costs. Since the Mark Twain Literacy Conference is held in Hannibal, our teachers can attend this conference at minimal expense. In addition, the Midwest chapter of T.A.W.L. (Teachers Applying Whole Language), based in Columbia, Missouri, has provided many wonderful conferences throughout the years. When they return from a conference, teachers share what they learned during the monthly coffees and at the workshops that are held each year before school opens.

Although not an inservice in the traditional sense, visits to classrooms both within the school and/or district and in other schools and districts can be extremely valuable. Many times an administrator will see a teacher struggling with an issue that another teacher in the building has already resolved. The administrator serves as a wonderful conduit for the good things that are happening in the school. Frequently the administrator can take over a teacher's class while she or he observes in other classrooms. This kind of inservice activity is very beneficial because the issues it addresses are specific to the needs of the teachers involved and because it enables the teachers to relate to one another in a more personal way. When teachers are encouraged to share rather than to compete with each other, the school's feeling of community is strengthened.

Another atypical form of inservice education occurs when teachers make presentations to other teachers. As teachers well know, one has to really understand something to be able to teach it. Having teachers teach other teachers benefits both the teachers in the audience and the teacher making the presentation. The teachers in the audience get firsthand information from teachers who have already experienced the trials and errors, the struggles, and the frustrations and successes of designing and implementing a whole language program. The teacher presenters, in turn, are provided with an opportunity to further internalize, solidify, and articulate their beliefs and practices. As Carol Brandt, a third-grade teacher at Oakwood, said after giving one presentation, "That was a great experience for someone who would not take high school speech because she didn't like to talk to her peers!"

The Role of the College or University in Professional Growth and Development

A Note from Elizabeth . . .
> *Enough cannot be said about the importance of the staff of a college or university serving as consultants for a school. At Oakwood, the University of Missouri has played an integral part in the development of a theory base from which to begin and maintain our move toward whole*

language. Dr. Dorothy Watson, professor of reading at the University of Missouri at Columbia, was brought in as a consultant by our central office to begin working with teachers in the Hannibal schools. From this relationship began the Mark Twain Literacy Conference, which has been held in Hannibal each year since then. Special guest speakers such as Jerry Harste, Kenneth Goodman, Ralph Peterson, Kittye Copeland, Carol Gilles, and others have attended the conference and contributed greatly to our professional growth and development. Teachers at Oakwood benefit from attending and from presenting at this conference.

Besides these special inservice activities and conferences, the Continuing Education Department of Missouri University has provided our staff with graduate courses. These courses have included Early Literacy Development, Children's Literature, and Assessment and Evaluation, to name a few. This support has been invaluable both to the teachers and to me as an administrator.

As we stated earlier, teachers must assume responsibility for becoming life-long learners. This is also true for professionals in teacher education. A critical part of this life-long learning for university personnel involves developing and maintaining close ties with schools and individual classrooms. Although our roles differ, classroom teachers, administrators, and university professors share common goals. We all want excellence in education for children and teachers alike. As teachers strive to implement new strategies, new methods, and new ways of being and doing in the classroom, their ongoing observations and analyses serve to inform teacher educators, thus impacting on future research and practice. Working together, teachers, administrators, and teacher educators can bring about changes that result in better education for all students.

A NOTE FROM KATHY . . .

During my years of tenure at Western Illinois University, I have had the great pleasure of working closely with a number of schools and school districts. Although I spend vast amounts of time in personal professional reading and study—working to keep abreast of new research and new methods and materials—it is the relationships with the individuals in these schools and school systems that have been the most essential ingredient in my own development as a teacher of teachers. From each individual . . . each relationship . . . I gain new insights into how children learn and develop into literate beings. I learn about how change evolves in classrooms, schools, and districts. And I learn more about myself as a learner, as a teacher, and as an agent of change.

From my work with Camille Breheny, an inspired kindergarten teacher, I have been able to learn more about the assessment of early literacy development and about the collaborative nature of learning in the kindergarten classroom. From Margaret Harn, a dedicated and fun-loving first-grade teacher and president of our Whole Language Support Group, I have learned about the importance of teacher empowerment. My work with Judy Lane, a creative and talented fifth-grade teacher, helped me see firsthand the effectiveness of a literature-based curriculum, reciprocal teaching, and the writing process at the middle school level. With Pam Whittington and Lynn Walwer I have enjoyed writing about strategies for early literacy development. With Sheila Shearer, Diane Fox, Karen Nudd, and Lila Gardner I have experienced the excitement of establishing a network and support group for teachers who are learning about and applying a whole language philosophy. The supervisors, administrators, and teachers in Quincy, London Mills, and Astoria, Illinois, have helped me learn the value of implementing long-term plans for staff development, and they have enriched my own professional growth and development in countless ways.

Finally, from the many, many students—both undergraduate and graduate—who have shared their knowledge and expertise through classroom discussions, projects, and presentations, I have gained immeasurable knowledge about the teaching and learning process. As the sign on my office door states: "I came to teach . . . I stayed to learn" (author unknown).

Professional Growth through Self-Study

In her book *Transitions,* Regie Routman, an experienced and widely esteemed whole language educator, discusses how she came to value self-study as an important and influential ingredient in her own professional growth and development. In the section entitled "On Becoming a Knowledgeable Teacher" she discusses how attending professional meetings and conferences and reading professional literature contributed significantly to her understanding and application of whole language philosophy. This is consistent with the discussion in chapter three about the teaching staff taking responsibility for its own development.

In the preceding section we discussed facilitating professional growth through contact with teacher educators and involvement in activities sponsored by educational organizations. In this section we emphasize professional reading and discuss ways administrators can engage teachers in thoughtful discussions about the literature.

Fortunately, there is an ever-growing list of good books about whole language. Authors of these books include well-known researchers and educators such as Don Holdaway, Donald Graves, Jane Hansen, Ken and Yetta Goodman, Lucy Calkins, Frank Smith, Constance Weaver, Ralph Peterson,

Maryann Eeds, Jerry Harste, Regie Routman, and Nancy Atwell, to name just a few. One of the most beneficial ways to spend school or district money is on good professional literature. A well-stocked professional library is a must in a whole language school. The books and journals there enable teachers, as well as administrators and other interested individuals, to stay current in the field and to gain both knowledge and practical ideas.

At Oakwood, textbook funds are used to buy professional books, and teachers spend some of their time at conferences looking for books that will be bought with school funds. In addition to books, professional journals such as *Phi Delta Kappan,* the *Reading Teacher, Language Arts, Childhood Education,* and *Young Children* are available in our professional library.

Supporting the Teacher as Researcher

Whole language educators view teaching as a continual learning process. Not surprisingly, whole language classrooms are often described as *dynamic* learning communities where teachers and students work collaboratively to identify problems, seek solutions, gain new knowledge, and apply new strategies for learning about and functioning in our world. The word *dynamic* suggests a classroom community that is full of energy. *Dynamic* also suggests motion or movement. It is both a powerful and an accurate descriptor for both the whole language classroom and the whole language teacher, who is committed to developing new understandings about the learning process.

Teachers' empowerment to take responsibility for their curriculum has naturally led to their taking responsibility for their own professional growth. While curriculum has typically been linked to staff development, the decisions concerning staff development have been made almost exclusively by administrators. As we discussed earlier, research supports teacher input into their own professional development. Conducting action research is one of the most powerful staff development activities in which a teacher can be involved. It is also an excellent vehicle for changing beliefs and teaching practices.

Whole language classrooms are fertile grounds for stimulating action research—research that is conducted *by the classroom teacher, in his or her own classroom, for his or her own purposes*. While there have been many successful collaborative research projects where teachers or teams of teachers work with an outside individual, such as a university professor, in designing and implementing classroom-based research, empowered teachers have begun to realize their own abilities and responsibilities insofar as asking critical questions and designing their own projects to seek answers to these questions.

Teachers for too long have been involved in practices that do not work well in the classroom. They have had, on more than one occasion, to demand that students read the basal selections and work the accompanying workbook and skill pack pages. They have struggled with content-area textbooks and seen the low retention rates in social studies and science. While they diligently administered and scored weekly spelling tests, they have seen students misspell these same words in their writing. Empowered teachers must have the freedom to discover best practices by creating hypotheses and then gathering the data to prove or disprove their hypotheses. An empowered teacher-researcher might ask, "Can modeling notetaking on an overhead projector improve how a child takes notes?" or "Can you begin to move fourth-graders away from an overuse of personal narrative in their writing by bringing it to their attention, then sharing other types of writing with them?" When teachers have a clear understanding of the behaviors and outcomes that they want students to achieve, they are in a better position to seek answers to meaningful questions that will result in positive classroom changes.

In order to foster self-confidence in conducting classroom research, teachers enrolled in a graduate course in early childhood reading methods are asked to apply any of several strategies discussed in class. Most of the options involve some degree of classroom research. For one week Pam Campbell, a first-grade teacher, decided to use children's literature rather than the adopted basal reader. She discusses how she went about conducting her experiment and what she found:

> For one week I provided children's literature for students to read other than their basal. Most of the literature selections were books I had previously read to the students; therefore, these were basically familiar pieces of literature. I purposely provided ten to fifteen books I had not read in class. Just as I predicted, the books I had read to the class were the books that children wanted most. From this observation, I confirmed my opinion that familiarity is important for young readers. This, in turn, gave me the support and encouragement I needed to read to the class as many books as possible each day. Prior to this activity I was only finding time to read one or two books each day. Now I read a minimum of four or five each day. I am amazed at how little time it takes and how wonderful these books are for transitional times.

Oftentimes the teacher-researcher will discover new and unexpected information. Such was the case for Pam:

> It was unbelievable how well the children's selections matched their own reading abilities. For example, I have one student who is completely a nonreader. On the first day this student found one of the four picture books I had purposely included just for him. I also

have two boys who are reading at about a fifth- or sixth-grade level. These boys went directly to the informational books. I couldn't have provided more appropriate material if I had made the choices myself.

From this activity I also found that students are able to stimulate great interest in literature among each other … far more than I could do alone. I heard students talking about what book each would chose for the next day. They were actually recommending books for one another based on their own reading choices.

Informed administrators can empower teachers to take responsibility for their own staff development by encouraging them to develop questions about their program and their students and to conduct classroom research to answer their questions. In this way, the administrator will be promoting not only effective and pertinent staff development but also lasting educational change. From Pam's experiment came the decision to continue using literature for the remainder of the school year. Additionally, she states, "I know not to wait until the end of the third quarter to start this activity next year!"

In the Preface of his book *Reclaiming the Classroom: Teacher Researcher as an Agency for Change,* Peter Medway describes empowered teachers who are functioning as researchers in their own classrooms. He states, "They become critical, responsive readers and users of current research, less apt to accept uncritically others' theories, less vulnerable to fad, and more authoritative in their assessment of curricula, methods, and materials." Here is a personal example of Medway's observations. Michelle, a teacher in a prekindergarten program who was enrolled in our graduate Early Childhood Reading course, was reading Bobbi Fisher's book *Joyful Learning.* In discussing her plans for a class project, Michelle referred to an oral reading checklist in Fisher's book. She said that while she liked the format of the checklist and the items included, she wanted a more in-depth assessment tool and therefore planned to revise the checklist to suit her own needs. Michelle's confidence as both a teacher and a researcher enabled her to develop and pilot what turned out to be a very valuable assessment instrument. An unempowered teacher would not have been comfortable doing what Michelle did—particularly when it involved a project for a graduate course!

A POSTSCRIPT FROM KATHY . . .

As we discussed earlier in this chapter, an important part of "staying whole" involves teachers' willingness to open themselves and their classrooms to further changes in both philosophy and classroom practices. In closing, I want to share a comment made by Joan McDearmon, a "master" preschool teacher:

> Even though I have grown very much in my beliefs about literacy, I still feel the need for further development of my personal philosophy about literacy. Routman stresses the need for that, and I do not believe I have fully developed mine yet. Perhaps it is something that is ever-changing.

> Both Elizabeth and I share with Joan the belief that to be a whole language teacher—to stay whole—involves a willingness to not only accept change but to embrace it. This is the challenge we share with whole language educators across the globe—to hold fast to our shared beliefs about a holistic approach to literacy, about the value of all learners, and about the importance of creating learning communities where individuals engage in meaningful study that is both joyous and fulfilling, while at the same time remaining open to new experiences, new learnings, and new understandings.

A POSTSCRIPT FROM ELIZABETH . . .

When teachers say, "I could never go back to the way I used to teach!" we are witnessing a true change in philosophy and in practice. At the base of that philosophy and practice is a fundamental dedication to continue the search for what works best for children. When we as administrators regard teachers the way teachers regard their students—appreciating and building on their strengths, acknowledging that self-evaluation is the best evaluation, and creating a democratic climate where cooperation and professionalism are nurtured—then we too become "teachers of teachers." When we have succeeded in creating whole language schools, we too will say, "I could never go back!"

References:

– **Fisher, B.** (1991). *Joyful learning: A whole language kindergarten.* Portsmouth, NH: Heinemann.
– **Medway, P.** (1987). (Ed) *Reclaiming the classroom: Teacher researcher as an agency for change.* Portsmouth, NH: Boynton/Cook Publishers.
– **Routman, R.** (1988). *Transitions: From literature to literacy.* Portsmouth, NH: Heinemann.
– **Watson, D., Burke, C., & Harste, J.** (1989). *Whole language: Inquiring voices.* New York: Scholastic.

Index